LAO
PHRASEBOOK

Joe Cummings

Lao phrasebook
2nd edition – February 2002

Published by
Lonely Planet Publications Pty Ltd, ABN 36 005 607 983
90 Maribyrnong St, Footscray, Victoria 3011, Australia

Lonely Planet Offices
Australia Locked Bag 1, Footscray, Victoria 3011
USA 150 Linden St, Oakland CA 94607
UK 10a Spring Place, London NW5 3BH
France 1 rue du Dahomey, 75011 Paris

Cover illustration
Follow that Jumbo! by Yukiyoshi Kamimura

ISBN 1 74059 168 2

text © Lonely Planet Publications Pty Ltd 2002
cover illustration © Lonely Planet Publications Pty Ltd 2002

Printed by The Bookmaker International Ltd
Printed in China

About the Author

After investing most of his youth strangling Stratocasters in dark bars, Joe Cummings ran away from home with the Peace Corps and discovered South-East Asia. Returning to his native USA, he earned meagre but steady cash as a professional student for several years, gaining two master's degrees, one in South-East Asian Studies/Thai Language and another in Applied Linguistics. He has also worked as a translator/interpreter of Thai, a Lao bilingual consultant in the USA and as a tour guide in Laos. Along the way, Joe hit the road for LP, writing the first editions of LP's *Thailand* and *Laos* guides, which he continues to update regularly. He has also authored LP's *Thai phrasebook, World Food: Thailand* and *Buddhist Stupas of Asia: The Shape of Perfection*. Joe visits Laos frequently from his home base in Thailand.

From the Author

I'm much indebted to a Lao friend who helped with the Lao script for this phrasebook, but who wished not to be mentioned by name. Thanks also to Steven Schipani, who facilitated many exchanges. For logistical support, I thank Oliver Bandmann of Baan Khily Gallery in Luang Prabang.

From the Publisher

The Mekong River flows the length of Laos and, in centuries past, has been explored and mapped by a bevy of crazy (mostly French) adventurers. And so the lure of Lao led Lonely Planet's Lingua crew back for a second time. This second expedition was mounted by Sally Steward, Peter D'Onghia and Ingrid Seebus in its early days, then commandeered by Jim Jenkin. Karina Coates and Karin Vidstrup Monk planned the imminent stages of departure and made short work of the dense jungle, thus guiding the team to new territory. Dogsbody Ben Handicott edited the scribe's account. Yukiyoshi Kamimura was expedition artist from cover to cover, and also charted the layout of the whole affair. Bruce Evans lent a learned eye to the itinerary, Sophie Putman was the invaluable trip jack-of-all-trades (master of many), Natasha Velleley plotted the map, Bibiana Jaramillo made sure it was all recorded in the correct typeface and Fabrice Rocher, another crazy Frenchman, provided his sparkling eyes and guaranteed a stylish, timely arrival at destination.

CONTENTS

6 Contents

HEALTH 133

SPECIFIC NEEDS 141

TIME, DATES & FESTIVALS 151

NUMBERS & AMOUNTS 161

EMERGENCIES 165

ENGLISH–LAO DICTIONARY 169

INDEX 217

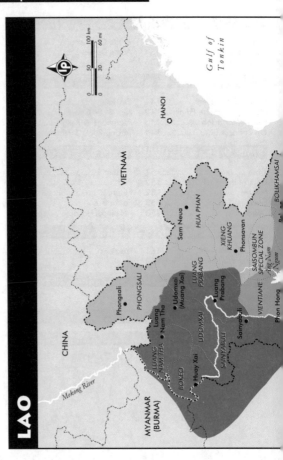

Map   9

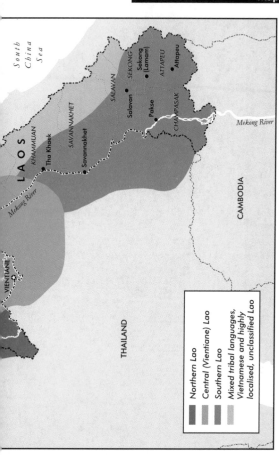

South
China
Sea

L A O S

KHAMMUAN

Tha Khaek

SAVANNAKHET

Savannakhet

SALAVAN

Salavan

SEKONG

Sekong
(Lamam)

ATTAPEU

Attapeu

Pakse

CHAMPASAK

Mekong River

Mekong River

VIENTIANE

THAILAND

CAMBODIA

Northern Lao

Central (Vientiane) Lao

Southern Lao

Mixed tribal languages,
Vietnamese and highly
localised, unclassified Lao

INTRODUCTION

The official language of the Lao People's Democratic Republic (LPDR) is Lao as spoken and written in Vientiane. As an official language, it has successfully become the lingua franca between all Lao and non-Lao ethnic groups in Laos. Of course, native Lao is spoken with differing tonal accents and with slightly differing vocabularies as you move from one part of the country to the next, especially in a north to south direction. But it is the Vientiane dialect that is most widely understood.

Modern Lao linguists recognise four basic dialects within the country: Vientiane Lao; Northern Lao (spoken in Sainyabuli, Bokeo, Udomxai, Phongsali, Luang Nam Tha and Luang Prabang); North-Eastern Lao (Xieng Khuang, Hua Phan), Central Lao (Khammuan, Bolikhamsai); and Southern Lao (Champasak, Salavan, Savannakhet, Attapeu, Sekong). Each of these can be further divided into subdialects; a distinction between the Lao spoken in the neighbouring provinces of Xieng Khuang and Hua Phan, for example, is readily apparent to those who know Lao well.

All dialects of Lao are members of the Thai half of the Thai-Kadai family of languages and are closely related to languages spoken in Thailand, northern Myanmar and pockets of China's Yunnan Province. Standard Lao is indeed close enough to Standard Thai (as spoken in central Thailand) that, for native speakers, the two are mutually intelligible. In fact, virtually all speakers of Lao living in the Mekong River Valley can easily understand spoken Thai, since the bulk of the television and radio they listen to is broadcast from Thailand. Among educated Lao, written Thai is also easily understood, in spite of the fact that the two scripts differ (to about the same degree that the Greek and Roman scripts differ). This is because many of the textbooks used at the college and university level in Laos are actually Thai texts.

INTRODUCTION

Even closer to Standard Lao are Thailand's Northern and North-Eastern Thai dialects. North-Eastern Thai (also called Isan) is virtually 100% Lao in vocabulary and intonation; in fact there are more Lao speakers living in Thailand than in Laos. Hence if you're travelling to Laos after a spell in Thailand (especially the north-east), you should be able to put whatever you learned in Thailand to good use in Laos. It doesn't work as well in the opposite direction; native Thais can't always understand Lao since they've had less exposure.

ABBREVIATIONS USED IN THIS BOOK

adj	adjective	pl	plural
adv	adverb	prep	preposition
conj	conjunction	sg	singular
lit	literal translation	v	verb
n	noun		

PRONUNCIATION

The rendering of Lao words into Roman script is a major problem, as many Lao sounds, especially certain vowels, do not occur in English. The problem is compounded by the fact that, because of Laos' colonial history, transcribed words most commonly seen in Laos are based on the colonial French system of transliteration, which bears little relation to the way an English speaker would usually choose to write a Lao word.

Take, for example, the capital of Laos, Vientiane. The Lao pronunciation, following a fairly logical English transliteration, would be Wieng Chan (some might hear it more as Wieng Jan). The French don't have a written consonant that corresponds to 'w', so they chose to use a 'v' to represent all 'w' sounds, even though the 'v' sound in Lao is closer to an English 'w'. The same goes for 'ch' (or 'j'), which for the French was best rendered 'ti-'; hence Wieng Chan comes out 'Vientiane' in the French transliteration. The 'e' is added so that the final 'n' sound isn't partially lost, as it is in French words ending with 'n'. This latter phenomenon also happens with words like lâan (ລ້ານ, million) as in Lan Xang, which most French speakers would write as 'Lane', a spelling that leads most English speakers to pronounce this word like the 'lane' in 'Penny Lane' (which is way off base).

As there is no official method of transliterating Lao (the Lao government is incredibly inconsistent in this respect, though they tend to follow the old French methods), we have created a transcription system similar to that used in Lonely Planet's *Thai phrasebook*, since the languages have a virtually identical sound system. The public and private sectors in Laos are gradually moving towards a more internationally recognisable system along the lines of the Royal Thai General Transcription (which is fairly readable across a large number of language types). This can also be problematic, however, as when an 'r' is used where an 'h' or 'l' is the actual sound, simply because the Lao symbols for these sounds look so much like the Thai 'r' (spoken Lao has no 'r' sound). Don't worry though, with our system, you'll be fine.

VOWELS

The x in the Lao script indicates the position that a consonant must fill to produce a written syllable.

x̍	i	as the 'i' in 'it'
x̂	ii	as the 'ee' in 'feet' or 'tea'
xະ, x̆x	a	as the 'u' in 'fun'
xๅ	aa	as the 'a' in 'father'
ແx	ae	as the 'a' in 'bat'
ເxະ, ເx̆x	e	as the 'e' in 'hen'
ເx	eh	as the 'a' in 'hate'
xຸ	u	as the 'u' in 'flute'
xູ	uu	as the 'oo' in 'food'
x̊, ອ	aw	as the 'aw' in 'jaw'
xํๅ	am	as the 'um' in 'rum'
ເx̂, ເx̂	oe	as the 'uh' in 'huh'
x̊, x̋	eu	similar to the 'i' in 'sir' or the 'eux' in the French 'deux'

Diphthongs		
ໄx, ໃx	ai	as the 'i' in 'pipe'
ເxๅ, xๅວ	ao	as the 'ow' in 'now'
ໂxະ, x̂	o	as the 'o' in 'phone'
ໂx	oh	as the 'o' in 'toe'
ເxຶອ	eua	combine eu and a
ເxຍ, ເxຍ, xງx	ia	combine i and a, or the 'ie' in the French 'rien'
x̂ວ	ua	as the 'our' in 'tour'
xວຍ	uay	as the 'ewey' in 'Dewey'
x̂ວ	iu	as the 'ew' in 'yew'
xງວ	iaw	similar to the 'io' in 'Rio'
ແxວ	aew	combine ae and w
ເxວ	ehw	combine eh and w
ເx̂ວ	ew	same as ehw above, but shorter
ເx̂ຍ	oei	combine oe and i
xອຍ	awy	combine aw and y

CONSONANTS

Some Lao consonant sounds may be represented by two separate characters, just as 'ph' and 'f' are pronounced the same way in English.

ສ, ຊ	s	as the 's' in 'soap'
ຝ, ຟ	f	same as the 'f' in 'fan'
ດ	d	as the 'd' in 'dodo'
ຕ	t	as the 't' in 'stop', similar to 'd'
ຖ, ທ	th	as the 't' as in 'tea'
ກ	k	as the 'k' in 'skin'
ຂ, ຄ	kh	as the 'k' in 'kite'
ບ	b	as the 'b' in 'boy'
ປ	p	as the 'p' in 'spin', similar to 'b'
ຜ, ພ	ph	as the 'p' in 'put' (but never as the 'ph' in 'phone')
ມ, ໝ	m	as the 'm' in 'man'
ນ, ໜ	n	as the 'n' in 'nun'
ງ	ng	as the 'ng' in 'sing'
ຍ	ny	similar to the 'ni' in 'onion'
ຈ	j	similar to the second 't' in 'stature'
ຢ	y	as the 'y' in 'yo-yo'
ລ, ຫຼ	l	as the 'l' in 'lick'
ວ	w	as the 'w' in 'wing'
ຫ, ຮ	h	as the 'h' in 'home'

PRONUNCIATION

PLAY IT AGAIN ...

ໆ	this character denotes repetition of the previous word

PRONUNCIATION

VARIATIONS IN TRANSLITERATIONS

In Laos you may come across many instances where the transliteration of vowels and consonants differs significantly, as in 'Louang' for Luang, 'Khouang' for Khuang or 'Xaignabouli' for Sainyabuli. The French spellings are particularly inconsistent in the use of the vowel 'ou', which in their transcriptions sometimes corresponds to a 'u' and sometimes to 'w'. An 'o' is often used for a short 'aw', as in 'Bo', which is pronounced more like baw.

Instances of 'v' in transcribed Lao words are generally pronounced more like a 'w'. For example, 'Vang Vieng' sounds more like Wang Wieng. In Vientiane, some of the older, educated upper class employ a strong 'v' rather than a 'w' sound.

Many standard place names in Roman script use an 'x' for what in English is 's'. There's no difference in pronunciation of the two; pronounce all instances of 'x' as 's'; for example, 'Xieng' should be pronounced sieng.

Finally, there's no 'r' sound in modern spoken Lao. When you see an 'r' in transcribed Lao, it's usually an old Lao or borrowed Thai transliteration; it should be pronounced like an 'l' in this case. Setthathirat (the name of a historic Lao king and common street name), for example, should actually be transcribed with an 'l' instead of an 'r' but usually isn't.

WIT & WISDOM

The wise man is a good listener.

| khón sá-làat nyáwm pen | ຄົນສະຫລາດຍອມ |
| khón hùu-ják fang | ເປັນຄົນຮູ້ຈັກຟັງ |

TONES

Traditionally, Lao is described as a monosyllabic, tonal language, like various forms of Thai and Chinese. Borrowed words from Sanskrit, Pali, French and English often have two or more syllables, however. Many syllables are differentiated by tone only. Consequently, the word sao, for example, can mean 'girl', 'morning', 'pillar' or 'twenty' depending on the tone. For people from non-tonal language backgrounds, this can take a bit of practice at first. Even when we 'know' the correct tone, our tendency to denote emotion, emphasis and questions through tone modulation often interferes with uttering the correct tone. So, the first rule in learning and using the tone system is to avoid overlaying your native intonation patterns onto Lao.

PRONUNCIATION

Vientiane Lao has six tones (compared with five in Standard Thai, four in Mandarin and up to nine in Cantonese). Three of the tones are level (low, mid and high) while three follow pitch inclines (rising, high falling and low falling). All six variations in pitch are relative to the speaker's natural vocal range, so that one person's low tone is not necessarily the same pitch as another person's. Hence, keen pitch recognition is not a prerequisite for learning a tonal language like Lao. A relative distinction between pitch contours is all that's necessary, just as it is with all languages (English and other European languages use intonation, too, just in a different way).

PRONUNCIATION

On a visual curve, the tones look like this:

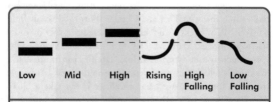

| Low | Mid | High | Rising | High Falling | Low Falling |

- The low tone is produced at the relative bottom of your conversational tonal range – usually flat and level (though not everyone pronounces it flat and level – some Vientiane natives add a slight rising tone to the end). For example, dii (ດີ, good).

- The mid tone is flat like the low tone, but spoken at the relative middle of the speaker's vocal range. No tone mark is used. For example, het (ເຮັດ, do).

- The high tone is flat again, this time at the relative top of your vocal range. For example, héua (ເຮືອ, boat).

- The rising tone begins a bit below the mid tone and rises to just at or above the high tone. For example, săam (ສາມ, three).

- The high falling tone begins at or above the high tone and falls to the mid level. For example, sào (ເຊົ້າ, morning).

- The low falling tone begins at about the mid level and falls to the level of the low tone. For example, khào (ເຂົ້າ, rice).

SCRIPT

This section will help those interested in learning about the fascinating, if somewhat complicated, Lao writing system. Fear not – if you're eager to hit the streets and speak Lao, skipping this section will not hinder your ability to communicate.

Prior to the consolidation of various Lao *méuang* (principalities) in the 14th century, there was little demand for a written language. When a written language was deemed necessary by the Lan Xang monarchy, Lao scholars based their script on an early alphabet devised by the Thais (which in turn had been created by Khmer scholars who used Mon scripts as models!). The alphabet used in Laos is closer to the original prototype; the original Thai script was later extensively revised (which is why Lao appears 'older' to orthographists than Thai, even though it's newer as a written language).

Before 1975, at least four spelling systems were in use. As modern printing never really established itself in Laos (most advanced textbooks being in Thai, French or Vietnamese before the revolution), Lao spelling wasn't standardised until after the Pathet Lao takeover. The current system has been highly simplified by omitting all literally transcribed spellings from foreign loan words. Instead of transliterating the Sanskrit *nagara* (city) letter for letter, for example, the new script uses only the letters actually pronounced in Lao, na-kháwn. Every letter written is pronounced, which means Lao script can be learned much more quickly than Thai or Khmer, both of which typically attempt to transcribe foreign borrowings letter for letter no matter what the actual pronunciation is.

Other scripts still in use include láo thám (dhamma Lao), used for writing Pali scriptures, and various Thai tribal scripts, the most popular and widespread being that of the Thai Neua (which has become standardised via Xishuangbanna, China).

The Lao script today consists of 28 consonants (but only 20 separate sounds) and 35 vowel and diphthong possibilities (16 separate symbols in varying combinations). In addition to the consonant and vowel symbols are four tone marks, only two of which are commonly used to create the six different tones (in combination with all the other symbols).

Written Lao proceeds from left to right, though vowel-symbols may be written before, above, below, 'around' (before, above and after) or after consonants, depending on the sign. Although learning the alphabet is not difficult, the writing system itself is fairly complex, so unless you're planning a lengthy stay in Laos, it should perhaps be foregone in favour of learning to actually speak the language.

How Spelling Determines Lao Tones

Several features combine to encode the correct tone for each word or syllable in written Lao. To begin with, all Lao consonants are divided into three 'classes': high, mid and low, each of which follows its own set of tone rules. Once you've established which consonant class begins the syllable, you look for the absence or presence of a tone mark over the initial consonant. Modern written Lao has two tone marks: the mâi èhk (´) and the mâi thóh (ˇ).

In standard Vientiane Lao, all syllables with a mâi èhk are spoken with the mid tone. Those with the mâi thóh are spoken with a low falling tone if they begin with a high-class consonant, or with a high falling tone if they begin with mid- or low-class consonants.

If there is no tone-mark over the syllable, then, in addition to knowing the consonant class, you must also take into consideration the length of the vowel and whether or not the word ends with that vowel or with a consonant. (This doesn't apply to tone-marked words, since they all end either with a vowel or with a nasal, ie, ng or n.)

Syllables with a stop final (p, t or k) combined with a long vowel take one set of tones (low falling for high- and mid-class consonants, high falling for low-class consonants), while those with short vowels take another (high tone for high- and mid-class consonants, mid tone for low-class consonants). In the case of short vowels without a final consonant, the tone is the same as for syllables with short vowels and stop finals.

For words of more than one syllable, each syllable has its own discrete tone, governed by the spelling of that syllable. Unlike Thai, there are no unwritten vowels in Lao, so the tone of one syllable never influences the following syllable – at least not in the written language.

The following charts show how these factors – consonant class, tone-mark, vowel length and syllable final – combine to encode the six tones in written Vientiane Lao. Although the system may seem rather complicated at first, once you've learned all the Lao characters, you can refer to these charts while learning to read and eventually internalise the Lao tone system.

Note that Lao dialects spoken in parts of Laos outside Vientiane Province follow their own tone rules. Also note that even the tone system for the Vientiane dialect is widely debated and true standardisation has yet to be achieved.

PRONUNCIATION

PRONUNCIATION

The Tonal System

Class	NTMNSF	mâi èhk	mâi thóh	SFLV	SFSV/SV
High	rising	mid	LF	LF	high
Mid	low	mid	HF	LF	high
Low	high	mid	HF	HF	mid

Examples with Transliteration

Class	NTMNS	mâi èhk	mâi thóh	SFLV	SFSV/SV
High	ຂາວ khǎo	ຂ່າວ khao	ເຂົ້າ khào	ຫຼວດ lâwt	ລົດ sót
Mid	ດີ dii	ຕ່າງ taang	ເຈົ້າ jâo	ຈອກ jàwk	ເດັກ dék
Low	ເງິນ ngóen	ນັ່ງ nang	ແລ້ວ lâew	ເລືອດ lêuat	ທຸກ thuk

Key:

LF = low falling
HF = high falling
SFSV/SV = stop final, short vowel;
  or short vowel, no final
  consonant

SFLV = stop final, long vowel
NTMNS = no tone mark, no
  stop final

GRAMMAR

The following outline provides an introduction to the basics of Lao grammar – it is not a complete description, but it provides the tools to start building your own Lao sentences for those conversations that lead off the beaten track.

WORD ORDER
In general, word order in Lao is very significant. For example, dâi (ໄດ້) placed immediately before the verb marks past tense, while the same word appearing immediately after the verb means 'can'.

Although the basic word order in Lao sentences is subject-verb-object, it's not uncommon to place the object first, for emphasis.

I don't like that bowl.
    thùay nân khàwy baw mak   ຖ້ວຍນັ້ນຂ້ອຍບໍ່ມັກ
    (lit: bowl that I no like)

NOUNS
Nouns never vary. They do not change to indicate plurality, and they do not need articles like 'a' or 'the'. Once you've learned the word for something, it stays the same. The word wat (ວັດ, temple), for example, never changes, no matter how many wat you're speaking about.

Verbs of physical action can be made into nouns by adding kạan (ການ) before the verb. Verbs describing abstract action – as well as adjectives – use khwáam (ຄວາມ) to form nouns.

to travel	dọen tháang	ເດີນທາງ
travel (n)	kạan dọen tháang	ການເດີນທາງ
to think	khit	ຄິດ
thought (n)	khwáam khit	ຄວາມຄິດ
good (adj)	dịi	ດີ
good (n)	khwáam dịi	ຄວາມດີ

23

ADJECTIVES

Lao adjectives always follow the nouns they modify, except in the
names of certain food dishes (eg, 'grilled chicken' is pîng kai, ປີ້ງໄກ່)
where the adjective precedes the noun. They don't change in any
way to 'agree' with the noun.

In Lao, you don't need to insert the verb 'to be' when describing
something. Instead of saying 'the house is red' as we do in English,
the Lao comes out as simply 'house red'.

big house
    héuan nyai   ເຮືອນໃຫຍ່
    (lit: house big)
delicious food
    kheuang kín sâep   ເຄື່ອງກິນແຊບ
    (lit: food delicious)
The room is small.
    hàwng nâwy   ຫ້ອງນ້ອຍ
    (lit: room small)

Comparatives

Basically any adjective in Lao can be used to make comparisons
by adding kwaa (ກ່ວາ) to it.

good	dįi	ດີ
better	dįi-kwaa	ດີກ່ວາ
cheap	thèuk	ຖຶກ
cheaper	thèuk-kwaa	ຖຶກກ່ວາ

Superlatives

Any adjective may be made superlative by adding thii-sút (ທີ່ສຸດ).

delicious	sâep	ແຊບ
the most delicious	sâep thii-sút	ແຊບທີ່ສຸດ
big	nyai	ໃຫຍ່
biggest	nyai thii-sút	ໃຫຍ່ທີ່ສຸດ

GRAMMAR

Equivalence

To express equivalence or sameness, use khéu káp (ຄືກັບ, the same as) or khéu kąn (ຄືກັນ, the same).

That kind is the same as this kind.
    sá-nit nân khéu káp sá-nit níi   ຊະນິດນັ້ນຄືກັບຊະນິດນີ້
    (lit: kind that khéu káp kind this)

Lao customs are not the same.
    pá-phéh-níi láo baw khéu kąn   ປະເພນີລາວບໍ່ຄືກັນ
    (lit: custom Lao no khéu kąn)

ADVERBS

Adjectives that can logically be used to modify action may function as adverbs in Lao. Usually this is indicated by doubling the adjective; this kind of adverb always follows the verb.

slow	sâa	ຊ້າ
slow horse	mâa sâa	ມ້າຊ້າ
	(lit: horse slow)	
Drive slowly.	kháp lot sâa-sâa	ຂັບລົດຊ້າໆ
	(lit: drive car slow-slow)	

Certain words and phrases function only as adverbs and, depending on the word or phrase, may either precede the verb or come at the end of the sentence.

Adverbs Before the Verb

ever	khóei	ເຄີຍ
never	baw khóei	ບໍ່ເຄີຍ
perhaps	bạng thíi	ບາງທີ
probably	àat já	ອາດຈະ
rarely	hǎa nyâak	ຫາຍຢາກ
sometimes	bạng theua	ບາງເທື່ອ
usually	pók-ká-tí	ປົກກະຕິ
yet; not yet	nyáng	ຍັງ

Adverbs at the End of a Sentence

also	khéu kạn	ຄືກັນ
always	lêuay lêuay	ເລື້ອຍໆ
immediately	thán thíi	ທັນທີ
often	lêuay	ເລື້ອຍ
only	thao-nân	ເທົ່ານັ້ນ

PRONOUNS
Demonstrative Pronouns

Demonstrative pronouns are the verbal equivalent of pointing.

Pronoun	with Noun	as a Question
this nîi ນີ້	this plate jạan nîi ຈານນີ້ (lit: plate nîi)	What's this? nîi maen nyăng ນີ້ແມ່ນຫຍັງ (lit: nîi be what)
that nân ນັ້ນ	that plate jạan nân ຈານນັ້ນ (lit: plate nân)	How much is that? nân thao-dại ນັ້ນເທົ່າໃດ (lit: nân equal what)
these lăo nîi ເຫຼົານີ້	these plates jạan lăo nîi ຈານເຫຼົານີ້ (lit: plate lăo nîi)	What are these? lăo nîi maen nyăng ເຫຼົານີ້ແມ່ນຫຍັງ (lit: lăo nîi be what)
those lăo nân ເຫຼົານັ້ນ	those plates jạan lăo nân ຈານເຫຼົານັ້ນ (lit: plate lăo nân)	How much are those? lăo nân thao-dại ເຫຼົານັ້ນເທົ່າໃດ (lit: lăo nân equal what)

Personal Pronouns

Lao has 10 common personal pronouns. They aren't used as frequently as their English equivalents since Lao is a 'subject-weak' language in which the subject of a sentence is often omitted after the first reference. There's no distinction between subject and object pronouns (ie, 'I' and 'me').

All Purpose Pronouns

The pronouns in this box will get you through your conversations, but as the opportunity arises, take the time to get to know some of the politer or more appropriate pronouns (some are given in the sections following) – they offer a little more insight into Lao culture.

I/me	khàwy	ຂ້ອຍ
he/she	khǎo	ເຂົາ
it	mán	ມັນ
you (sg)	jâo	ເຈົ້າ
you (pl)	phûak jâo	ພວກເຈົ້າ
we	phûak háo	ພວກເຮົາ
us	phûak khàwy	ພວກຂ້ອຍ
they	phûak khǎo	ພວກເຂົາ

GRAMMAR

First Person – I/We

I/me (to most people)
  khàwy   ຂ້ອຍ
I/me (when speaking to elders or people with high status)
  kháa-nâwy   ຂ້ານ້ອຍ
we/us
  phûak háo; phûak khàwy   ພວກເຮົາ/ພວກຂ້ອຍ
  (lit: group we; group us)

Second Person – You

you (sg)	jâo	ເຈົ້າ
you (pl)	phûak jâo	ພວກເຈົ້າ
	(lit: group you)	

The general all-purpose 'you' is jâo.

The pronoun thaan (ທ່ານ) is reserved for people in high social positions such as monks or government officials. You may also use it with Lao who are substantially older than you to show respect, although jâo is sufficient.

Other Terms of Address

Other terms of address you may hear, but probably won't use, include:

lúng	ລຸງ	to an older man (lit: uncle)
pâa	ປ້າ	to an older woman (lit: aunt)
toh	ໂຕ	to a lover or other intimate relation
êuay	ເອື້ອຍ	to a female or social equal (lit: older sister)
âai	ອ້າຍ	to a male or social equal (lit: older brother)
nâwng	ນ້ອງ	to someone of any gender younger than you (lit: younger sibling)

None of these kinship terms is appropriate for use by a foreigner with an elementary command of Lao.

GRAMMAR

Third Person – He/She/It/They

he/she (when speaking of most people)
   khǎo   ເຂົາ

he/she (when speaking of elders or monks)
   phoen   ເພິ່ນ

he/she (when speaking about people you know)
   láo   ລາວ

he/she (when speaking about persons with high status)
   thaan   ທ່ານ

it (inanimate objects and animals)
   mán   ມັນ

they
   phûak added before khǎo, láo   ພວກ
   or phoen as with 'you' (plural)

In general, khǎo is the all-encompassing term; there is no gender or number distinction. When speaking of people you know personally, láo can be used, though for elders phoen is better. For monks phoen should be substituted (same as for second-person) to express respect. For example:

How many months has he been a monk?
   phoen bùat pen khúu-baa   ເພິ່ນບວດເປັນຄູບາໄດ້
   dâi ják dẹuan lâew   ຈັກເດືອນແລ້ວ
   (lit: phoen ordain be monk
      how many month already)

GRAMMAR

POSSESSION

Khǎwng (ຂອງ) is used to denote possession and is roughly equivalent to the preposition 'of' or the verb 'belongs to' in English.

my bag
    thǒng khǎwng khàwy   ຖົງຂອງຂ້ອຍ
    (lit: bag khǎwng I)
his/her seat
    bawn nang khǎwng láo   ບ່ອນນັ່ງຂອງລາວ
    (lit: place sit khǎwng he/she)
Does this belong to you?
    nîi máen khǎwng jâo baw   ນີ້ແມ່ນຂອງເຈົ້າບໍ່
    (lit: this be khǎwng you no)

The ever-versatile khǎwng can also be used as a noun to mean 'stuff' or 'things'.

She went to buy some things.
    khǎo pai sêu kheuang khǎwng   ເຂົາໄປຊື້ເຄື່ອງຂອງ
    (lit: she go buy some khǎwng)

For 'whose' use khǎwng phǎi (ຂອງໃຜ, belong who).

Whose plate is this?
    jaan nîi maen khǎwng phǎi   ຈານນີ້ແມ່ນຂອງໃຜ
    (lit: plate this be khǎwng phǎi)

VERBS

Tense

Lao verbs do not change their spellings or pronunciations to account for time references. Time is conveyed by context and by means of adding time indicators like 'today', 'tomorrow', 'yesterday', 'last year'and so on, or by adding markers that indicate ongoing action, completed action and to-be-completed action.

Out of context, without a time reference, the sentence láo kịn kai (ລາວກິນໄກ່) could mean 'She/He eats/ate/has eaten/will eat chicken'.

Adding mêu-wáan-nîi (ມື້ວານນີ້, yesterday) to the sentence, as in mêu-wáan-nîi láo kịn kai (ມື້ວານນີ້ລາວກິນໄກ່), gives this sentence a definite 'past' sense. Likewise mêu-nîi (ມື້ນີ້, today) láo kịn kai gives it a 'present' sense.

As in English, the time sense can be further qualified by the addition of words like 'often', 'seldom', 'every day', etc.

Ongoing Action

Verbs used in the absence of time markers such as 'yesterday' and 'tomorrow', are usually taken to indicate present or ongoing action.

They are playing guitar.
    phûak khǎo lìn kịi-tạa   ພວກເຂົາຫລິ້ນກິຕາ
    (lit: group he/she play guitar)

GRAMMAR

WIT AND WISDOM

If you are shy with the teacher you won't learn;
if you are shy with women you won't get married.
    qai khúu baw dâi khwáam   ອາຍຄູບໍ່ໄດ້ຄວາມຮູ້ ອາຍ
    hûu qai sûu baw dâi mía   ຊູ້ບໍ່ໄດ້ເມຍ

Completed Action

The most common way of expressing completed action in Lao is by adding the past tense word lâew (ແລ້ວ) after the verb (if there is no direct or indirect object; after the object otherwise).

We went to Vientiane.
 phûak khàwy pại wíeng jạn lâew   ພວກເຮົາໄປວຽງຈັນແລ້ວ
 (lit: group I go Vientiane lâew)
I spent the money.
 khàwy jai ngóen lâew   ຂ້ອຍຈ່າຍເງິນແລ້ວ
 (lit: I spend money lâew)

Note that, as in the last example above, lâew can refer to a current condition that began in the immediate past.

Dâi (ໄດ້, to be able) also shows past tense but, unlike lâew, it's never used with present action. It immediately precedes the verb, and is often used in conjunction with lâew. It is more commonly employed in negative statements than in the affirmative.

Our friends didn't go to
Luang Prabang.
 pheuan phûak háo baw   ເພື່ອນພວກເຮົາບໍ່ໄດ້
 dâi pại lŭang pha-bạng   ໄປຫລວງພະບາງ
 (lit: friend group we no dâi go
 Luang Prabang)

To-Be-Completed Action

The future markers já (ຈະ) or sii (ຊີ) are used to mark an action to be completed in the future. It always appears directly before the verb.

She/He will buy rice.
 láo já sêu khào   ລາວຈະຊື້ເຂົ້າ
 (lit: she/he já buy rice)

Making Requests & Giving Commands

Khǎw (ຂໍ), a word that cannot be directly translated into English, is used to make polite requests. Depending on the context, it's roughly equivalent to 'please give me' or 'may I ask for'. Khǎw always comes at the beginning of a sentence, and is often used in conjunction with the added 'politener' dae (ແດ່) – spoken at the end of the sentence.

> Please pass some rice.
> khǎw khào dae   ຂໍເຂົ້າແດ່
> (lit: khǎw rice dae)

If you want someone to do something, you can politely preface the sentence with khǎw suay (ຂໍຊ່ວຍ, 'May I ask help?') or sóen (ເຊີນ, 'I invite you'). In English the closest equivalent is 'please'.

> Please close the window.
> khǎw suay pít pawng îam dae   ຂໍຊ່ວຍປິດປ່ອງອ້ຽມແດ່
> (lit: khǎw suay help close
>   window dae)

> Please sit down.
> sóen nang   ເຊີນນັ່ງ
> (lit: sóen sit)

To express a greater sense of urgency, use dòe (ເດີ້) at the end of a sentence.

> Close the door.
> pít pá-tuu dòe   ປິດປະຕູເດີ້
> (lit: close door dòe)

TO BE

The verb 'to be' in Lao is much more limited in function than its English counterpart. There are two forms – maen (ແມ່ນ) and pẹn (ເປັນ) – which are only used to join nouns and/or pronouns. They are not used to join nouns or pronouns with adjectives (see Adjectives, page 24).

As a rule, use maen for objects and pẹn for people.

This is a pedicab.
 ạn-nǐi maen sǎam-lâw   ອັນນີ້ແມ່ນສາມລໍ້
 (lit: this maen pedicab)

I'm a musician.
 khàwy pẹn nak-dọn-tịi   ຂ້ອຍເປັນນັກດົນຕີ
 (lit: I pẹn musician)

Pẹn is also used to show ability (see Can, page 38) and and can as well mean 'to have' when describing a person's condition (see To Have, page 35).

If you want to say 'there is ...' or 'there are ...', the verb mǐi (ມີ, 'to have') is used instead of pẹn. Mǐi here means 'to have' in the sense of 'to exist' – you're likely to hear it in sentences like:

In Vientiane, there are many cars.
 yuu wiéng jạn mǐi lot lǎai   ຢູ່ວຽງຈັນມີລົດຫລາຍ
 (lit: stay Vientiane mǐi car many)

There's a large Buddha image at
Wat Ong Teu.
 wat ọng têu mǐi   ວັດອົງຕື້ມີ
 pha-phut-tha-hûup nyai   ພະພຸດທະຮູບໃຫຍ່
 (lit: Wat Ong Teu mǐi
   Buddha-image big)

TO HAVE

Míi (ມີ) means 'to have' and, as mentioned on page 34, can also be used to mean 'there is' or 'there are'.

I have a bicycle.
    khàwy míi lot thìip   ຂ້ອຍມີລົດຖີບ
    (lit: I míi vehicle pedal)
Do you have fried rice noodles?
    míi phát fŏe baw   ມີຜັດເຝິ່
    (lit: míi fry rice-noodle no)

Pẹn, 'to be', is used in the sense of 'to have' when describing a person's condition.

I have a fever.
    khàwy pen khài   ຂ້ອຍເປັນໄຂ້
    (lit: I pẹn fever)

She/He has a cold.
    láo pẹn wát   ລາວເປັນຫວັດ
    (lit: she/he pẹn common-cold)

GRAMMAR

GRAMMAR DOESN'T RULE!

Grammar rules are certainly made to be broken – don't be afraid to experiment with some of the phrases and formulas you find in this section. Communicate in any way you can, string words together and don't hesitate to create a few 'interesting' sentences! The finer points will come ...

NEGATIVES

Baw (ບໍ່, no) is the main negative marker in Lao. Nyáng (ຍັງ) is also
used to mean 'not yet' in answer to questions that end in lâew baw
(ແລ້ວບໍ່, see Questions, page 39). Nyáng is placed before baw in a
complete sentence, or alone to mean simply 'Not yet'.

Any verb or adjective may be negated by the insertion of baw
immediately before it.

She/He isn't thirsty.
    láo baw yàak nâm   ລາວບໍ່ຢາກນ້ຳ
    (lit: she/he baw want water)
I don't have any cash.
    khàwy baw míi ngóen   ຂ້ອຍບໍ່ມີເງິນ
    (lit: I baw have money)
We're not French.
    phûak háo baw pęn   ພວກເຮົາບໍ່ເປັນຄົນຝະລັ່ງ
    khón fa-lang
    (lit: group we baw be people French)
John has never gone to Savannaket.
    john baw khóei   ຈອນບໍ່ເຄີຍໄປ
    pại sa-wăn-na-khèt   ສະຫວັນນະເຂດ
    (lit: John baw ever go
        Savannaket)
We won't go to Pakse tomorrow.
    mêu eun phûak háo   ມື້ອື່ນພວກເຮົາ
    baw pại pàak-séh   ບໍ່ໄປປາກເຊ
    (lit: day other group we
        baw go Pakse)
You haven't eaten yet.
    jâo nyáng baw thán kịn khào   ເຈົ້າຍັງບໍ່ທັນກິນເຂົ້າ
    (lit: you nyáng baw yet eat rice)

MODALS

Like most other languages, Lao makes use of words like 'should', 'want to', 'need to' or 'can' in conjunction with verbs to express obligation, want/need and ability (eg, must do, need to do, can do').

Obligation

Khúan (ຄວນ) serves as 'should' or 'ought to', usually in conjunction with jà, the marker for to-be-completed action.

You should eat.
    jào khúan já kĭn khào   ເຈົ້າຄວນຈະກິນເຂົ້າ
    (lit: you khúan já eat rice)
She/He shouldn't do that.
    láo baw khúan hét naew nân   ລາວບໍ່ຄວນເຮັດແນວນັ້ນ
    (lit: she/he no khúan do like that)

Want

Yàak (ຢາກ) is placed in front of the verb to express 'want' or 'desire'.

The dog wants to eat.
    mǎa yàak kĭn khào   ໝາຢາກກິນເຂົ້າ
    (lit: dog yàak eat rice)
I don't want to walk.
    khàwy baw yàak nyaang   ຂ້ອຍບໍ່ຢາກຍ່າງ
    (lit: I no yàak walk)

When 'want' is used with a noun, it takes the form of either ạo (ເອົາ, take) or yàak dâi (ຢາກໄດ້, want to get).

I want bananas.
    khàwy ạo kûay   ຂ້ອຍເອົາກ້ວຍ
    (lit: I ạo banana)
Tom wants a shirt.
    thawm yàak dâi sèua   ທອມຢາກໄດ້ເສື້ອ
    (lit: Tom yàak dâi shirt)

Need

The word tâwng (ຕ້ອງ) comes before verbs to mean 'must' or 'need to'. When using 'need' plus a noun, use tâwng-kạan (ຕ້ອງການ).

> I must go to the market.
> > khàwy tâwng pại tá-làat   ຂ້ອຍຕ້ອງໄປຕະຫລາດ
> > (lit: I tâwng go market)

> We need to look for a house.
> > háo tâwng hǎa héuan   ເຮົາຕ້ອງຫາເຮືອນ
> > (lit: we tâwng seek house)

> You don't have to stay here.
> > jâo baw tâwng phák yuu-nîi   ເຈົ້າບໍ່ຕ້ອງພັກຢູ່ນີ້
> > (lit: you no tâwng stay here)

> I need a bicycle.
> > khàwy tâwng-kạan lot-thìip   ຂ້ອຍຕ້ອງການລົດຖີບ
> > (lit: I tâwng-kạan bicycle)

Can

Lao has three ways of expressing 'can': dâi, pẹn and sǎa-màat. Dâi (ໄດ້) means 'to be able to' or 'to be allowed to' and is the more general equivalent of the English 'can'. It always follows the verb (and negative marker and object, if any).

> Can you go?
> > pại dâi baw   ໄປໄດ້ບໍ່
> > (lit: go dâi no)

> I can't go.
> > pại baw dâi   ໄປບໍ່ໄດ້
> > (lit: go no dâi)

> I can't eat pork.
> > kịn sîin mǔu baw dâi   ກິນຊີ້ນໝູບໍ່ໄດ້
> > (lit: eat piece pig no dâi)

Pẹn (ເປັນ) may mean 'can' in the sense of 'to know how to'. Like dâi, it ends the verb phrase.

> She/He knows how to play guitar.
> láo lìn kịi-tạa pẹn ລາວຫລິ້ນກີຕາເປັນ
> (lit: she/he play guitar pẹn)

Sǎa-màat (ສາມາດ) is used as 'can' to express physical possibility or ability. Unlike dâi and pẹn, it's placed before the verb.

> I can't lift that.
> khàwy baw sǎa-màat nyok ຂ້ອຍບໍ່ສາມາດຍົກ
> an-nân kèun ອັນນັ້ນຂຶ້ນ
> (lit: I no sǎa-màat lift classifier-that up)

QUESTIONS

Lao has two ways of forming questions: use of a question word like 'who', 'how', 'what', etc or through the addition of a tag like 'isn't it?' or 'no?' to the end of the sentence.

Many English-speakers instinctively place an English question inflection to the end of a Lao question; try to avoid doing this as it will usually throw off the Lao tones.

Question Words

Note the placement of Lao question words in a sentence. Some come at the beginning of the question, others at the end.

What?	nyǎng	ຫຍັງ

> What do you need?
> jâo tawng-kạan nyǎng ເຈົ້າຕ້ອງການຫຍັງ
> (lit: you need nyǎng)

How?	náew-dại	ແນວໃດ
	(lit: manner which)	

> How do you do it?
> hét náew-dại ເຮັດແນວໃດ
> (lit: do náew-dại)

Who?	phǎi	ໃຜ

Who's sitting there?
phǎi nang yuu hân   ໃຜນັ່ງຢູ່ຫັ້ນ
(lit: phǎi sit stay there)

When?	wéh-láa dại	ເວລາໃດ
	(lit: time which)	

When will you go to Luang Prabang?
wéh-láa dại já pại   ເວລາໃດຈະໄປ
lǔang pha-bạng   ຫລວງພະບາງ
(lit: wéh-láa dại future-marker
go Luang Prabang)

Why?	pẹn nyǎng	ເປັນຫຍັງ
	(lit: be what)	

Why are you so quiet?
pẹn nyǎng jâo mit thâe   ເປັນຫຍັງເຈົ້າມິດແທ້
(lit: pẹn nyǎng you quiet real)

How much?	thâo dại	ເທົ່າໃດ
	(lit: equal what)	

How much is this?
nîi thao dại   ນີ້ເທົ່າໃດ
(lit: this thâo dại)

Where?	yuu sǎi	ຢູ່ໃສ
	(lit: stay where)	

Where's the bathroom?
hàwng nâam yuu sǎi   ຫ້ອງນ້ຳຢູ່ໃສ
(lit: room water yuu sǎi)

GRAMMAR

Which?	an dại	ອັນໃດ
	(lit: classifier which)	

Which one do you like?
jâo mak an dại   ເຈົ້າມັກອັນໃດ
(lit: you like an dại)

Tags

Just like in English, a 'tag' comes at the end of a sentence and requests confirmation of what has been proposed in that same sentence.

isn't it?/is it?	baw	ບໍ່

The weather's hot, isn't it?
ạa-kàat hâwn baw   ອາກາດຮ້ອນບໍ່
(lit: air hot baw)

right?	maen baw	ແມ່ນບໍ່

You're a writer, right?
jâo pẹn nak-khían maen baw   ເຈົ້າເປັນນັກຂຽນແມ່ນບໍ່
(lit: you be student maen baw)

or not?	lěu baw	ຫລືບໍ່

Do you want to go out or not?
yàak pại lìn lěu baw   ຢາກໄປຫລິ້ນຫລືບໍ່
(lit: want go play lěu baw)

yet?	lâew baw	ແລ້ວບໍ່

Have you eaten yet?
jâo kịn khào lâew baw   ເຈົ້າກິນເຂົ້າແລ້ວບໍ່
(lit: you eat rice lâew baw)

eh?	lěu	ຫລື

ANSWERS

To answer questions in Lao, you merely repeat the verb, with or without the negative particle baw (ບໍ່). Informally, a negative particle will do for a negative reply.

Do you want to drink tea?	yàak kin nâm sáa baw (lit: want eat water tea no)	ຍາກກິນນ້ຳຊາບໍ່
Yes.	yàak kin (lit: want eat)	ຍາກກິນ
No.	baw yàak kin (lit: no want eat)	ບໍ່ຍາກກິນ
Are you well?	sá-baai-dii baw (lit: well no)	ສະບາຍດີບໍ່
Yes.	sá-baai-dii (lit: well)	ສະບາຍດີ
No.	baw sá-baai (lit: no well)	ບໍ່ສະບາຍ
Have you eaten yet?	kin khào lâew baw (lit: eat rice already no)	ກິນເຂົ້າແລ້ວບໍ່
Yes.	kin lâew (lit: eat already)	ກິນແລ້ວ
No.	nyáng (lit: yet)	ຍັງ
You're a teacher, aren't you?	jâo pen khúu maen baw (lit: you be teacher be no)	ເຈົ້າເປັນຄູແມ່ນບໍ່
Yes.	maen (lit: be)	ແມ່ນ
No.	baw maen (lit: no be)	ບໍ່ແມ່ນ
Are you happy?	dii-jai lěu baw (lit: happy or no)	ດີໃຈຫຼືບໍ່
Yes.	dii-jai (lit: happy)	ດີໃຈ
No.	baw (lit: no)	ບໍ່

GRAMMAR

CLASSIFIERS

Classifiers or counters are words which define the category that an item being counted belongs to. These are comparable to words like 'slice' and 'sheet' in English (as in 'two slices of bread' or 'three sheets of paper').

To state a quantity of something in Lao, you first name the thing you want, then the number and finally the classifier or counter of the item – so five oranges is màak-kîang hàa nuay (ໝາກກ້ຽງຫ້າໜ່ວຍ, orange five classifier). Every noun that's countable in Lao takes a classifier.

Common Classifiers

animals, furniture, clothing	tǫh	ໂຕ
candles, books	hǔa	ຫົວ
Buddha images	ǫng	ອົງ
buses, cars, bikes, vehicles	khán	ຄັນ
fruit, balls	nuay	ໜ່ວຍ
glasses (of water, tea, etc)	jàwk	ຈອກ
houses	lǎng	ຫລັງ
letters, newspapers (flatsheets)	sá-báp	ສະບັບ
monks	hùup	ຮູບ
pairs of items (people, things)	khuu	ຄູ່
people	khón	ຄົນ
pills, seeds, small gems	kaen	ແກ່ນ
plates (food)	jaan	ຈານ
rolls (toilet paper, film)	mûan	ມ້ວນ
round hollow objects, leaves	bai	ໃບ
sets of things	sut	ຊຸດ
slices (cakes, cloth)	phaen	ແຜ່ນ
small objects, miscellaneous	tǫh	ໂຕ

GRAMMAR

If you don't know (or forget) the appropriate classifier, tǫh (ໂຕ) may be used for almost any small thing. Alternatively, the Lao sometimes repeat the noun rather than not use a classifier at all.

PREPOSITIONS

above	tháang thóeng	ທາງເທິງ
across from	khâam káp	ຂ້າມກັບ
adjacent to	yuu khàang káp	ຢູ່ຂ້າງກັບ
around	hâwp	ຮອບ
at	yuu	ຢູ່
behind	tháang lăng	ທາງຫລັງ
beside	tháang khàang	ທາງຂ້າງ
from	tae	ແຕ່
in (and inside)	nái	ໃນ
in front of	tháang nàa	ທາງໜ້າ
of	khăwng	ຂອງ
on	thóeng	ເທິງ
opposite	kong kạn khâam káp	ກົງກັນຂ້າມກັບ
under	kàwng	ກ້ອງ
with	káp/nám	ກັບ/ນຳ

CONJUNCTIONS

and	lae	ແລະ
because	phaw waa	ເພາະວ່າ
but	tae waa	ແຕ່ວ່າ
or	lĕu waa	ຫລືວ່າ
since	tâng tae	ຕັ້ງແຕ່
so (therefore)	phaw sá-nân	ເພາະສະນັ້ນ
so that (in order to)	pheua	ເພື່ອ
then	lâew	ແລ້ວ
when	mêua/wéh-láa	ເມື່ອ/ເວລາ

GRAMMAR

The all-purpose Lao greeting (and farewell) is sa-ḅaai-dịi (ສະບາຍດີ). It's often accompanied by a nop (ນົບ), the palms-together gesture of respect, or by a light handshake. If someone says sá-ḅaai-dịi to you, you should reply with the same phrase. A smile and sá-ḅaai-dịi goes a long way toward calming the initial trepidation that locals may feel upon seeing a foreigner, whether in the city or the countryside.

YOU SHOULD KNOW   ໜ້າຈະຮູ້

How are you?	sá-ḅaai-dịi baw	ສະບາຍດີບໍ່
I'm fine.	sá-ḅaai-dịi	ສະບາຍດີ
Thank you.	khàwp jại	ຂອບໃຈ
And you?	jâo dẹh	ເຈົ້າເດ
Thank you very much.	khàwp jại lǎi lǎi	ຂອບໃຈຫລາຍໆ
It's nothing.	baw pẹn nyǎng	ບໍ່ເປັນຫຍັງ
(never mind; don't bother)		
Excuse me.	khǎw thôht	ຂໍໂທດ

IT'S ALL IN THE HANDS

Traditionally the Lao greet each other not with a handshake but with a prayer-like, palms-together gesture known as a nop (ນົບ). If someone nop-s you, you should nop back (unless nop-ed by a child). In Vientiane and large cities, a light version of the Western-style handshake is commonly offered to foreigners.

To beckon someone to come towards you, wave your hand with the palm down. This same gesture can be used to hail public transport along the side of the road.

A quick lifting of the eyebrows is often used to express affirmation or consent.

GREETINGS ການທັກທາຍ

As well as sá-baai-dji, other common greetings – especially when meeting someone on the road – are pai săi (ໄປໃສ, 'Where are you going?') and kǐn khào lâew baw (ກິນເຂົ້າແລ້ວບໍ່, 'Have you eaten yet?'). As with the English 'How are you?', the answer doesn't usually matter. If you're just out for a stroll, a common reply to pai săi is nyaang lín (ຍ່າງຫລິ້ນ), which roughly translates into 'I'm just walking for fun'.

The greeting kin kháo lâew baw carries an implicit invitation to dine together (even for just a quick bowl of noodles), hence you choose the reply based on whether you'd like to spend time with the greeter. Answer nyáng (ຍັງ, 'Not yet') if you're willing to accept a possible meal invitation; answer kin lâew (ກິນແລ້ວ, 'I've eaten already'), if you'd rather be on your way.

GOODBYES ລາກ່ອນ

As mentioned, a simple sá-baai-dji can be used as a farewell, especially if both speakers are leaving at the same time.

If you are leaving and the person you're speaking to is staying behind, you can say láa kawn (ລາກ່ອນ, 'leaving first') or pai káwn (ໄປກ່ອນ, 'going first'). If you're the one staying, you bid farewell by saying sôhk dji (ໂຊກດີ, 'good luck').

Whether you're staying or going, it can also be appropriate to say phop kạn mai (ພົບກັນໃໝ່), meaning 'We'll meet again' (roughly equivalent to 'See you later').

FORMS OF ADDRESS ການຢຽກເອີ້ນ

The Lao generally address each other using their first names with a kinship term or other title preceding it. Other formal terms of address include thaan (ທ່ານ, Mr) and náang (ນາງ, Miss or Mrs). Friends often use nicknames or kinship terms like âai/êuay (elder brother/sister), nâwng (younger sibling) or lúng/pâa (uncle/aunt) depending on the age differential. Young children can be called lăan (nephew or niece).

The following list includes kinship terms commonly used as forms of address for non-family members, based on relative age difference from the speaker. For more kinship terms, see Family on page 52.

elder sister	êuay	ເອື້ອຍ
elder brother	âai	ອ້າຍ
younger sibling	nâwng	ນ້ອງ
grandmother	mae thào	ແມ່ເຖົ້າ
grandfather	phaw thào	ພໍ່ເຖົ້າ
aunt	pâa	ປ້າ
uncle	lúng	ລຸງ
niece/nephew	lǎan	ຫລານ

BODY LANGUAGE ພາສາໂບ້ຍ

Non-verbal behaviour is very important in Laos, perhaps more important than in most Western countries.

When walking indoors in front of someone who's sitting down, you should stoop a little as a sign of respect.

The feet are the lowest part of the body (spiritually as well as physically) so don't point your feet at people or point at things with your feet. In the same context, the head is regarded as the highest part of the body, so don't touch the Lao on the head either.

SIN-FUL

Wearing clothes that bare the thighs, shoulders or breasts is often perceived as improper or disrespectful behaviour in Laos. Long trousers and walking shorts for men and women, as well as skirts, are acceptable attire. Tank tops, sleeveless blouses and short skirts or shorts are not. Many visiting women find that the traditional Lao sìn, a long patterned skirt, makes fine travel wear. For Lao women, such dress is mandatory for visits to government offices and museums.

MEETING PEOPLE

FIRST ENCOUNTERS ການປະເສິບໜ້າຄັ້ງທຳອິດ

What's your name?
jâo seu nyăng ເຈົ້າຊື່ຫຍັງ
My name is ...
khàwy seu ... ຂ້ອຍຊື່ ...
Glad to know you.
nyín dji thii dâi hûu-ják ຍິນດີທີ່ໄດ້ຮູ້ຈັກ

MAKING CONVERSATION ການສືບທະບາໆ

We're friends.
háo pẹn pheuan kạn ເຮົາເປັນເພື່ອນກັນ
We're relatives.
háo pẹn phii-nâwng kạn ເຮົາເປັນພີ່ນ້ອງກັນ
I've come on business.
khàwy máa het thu-la-kít ຂ້ອຍມາເຮັດທຸລະກິດ
I've come on pleasure.
khàwy máa thîaw ຂ້ອຍມາທ່ຽວ
Nice weather, isn't it?
aa-káat dji maen baw ອາກາດດີແມ່ນບໍ່
It's quite hot in Laos.
meúang láo hâwn lăai ເມືອງລາວຮ້ອນຫລາຍ
I like it here.
khàwy mak yuu nîi ຂ້ອຍມັກຢູ່ນີ້
May I have your address?
khăw thii-yuu khăwng ຂໍທີ່ຢູ່ຂອງເຈົ້າໄດ້ບໍ່
jâo dâi baw
This is my address.
nîi maen thii-yuu ນີ້ແມ່ນທີ່ຢູ່ຂອງຂ້ອຍ
khăwng khàwy

address	thii-yuu	ທີ່ຢູ່
fluent	lian lăai	ຫລຽບໄຫລ
friend	pheuan	ເພື່ອນ
language	pháa-săa	ພາສາ
phone number	nám-bọe thóh-la-sáp	ນາໝເບີ້ໂທລະສັບ
study/learn	hían	ຮຽນ

BREAKING THE LANGUAGE BARRIER

ຄວາມຫຍຸ້ງຫຍາກ
ດ້ານພາສາ

I can't speak (much) Lao.
khàwy pàak pháa-săa
láo baw dâi (lăai)

ຂ້ອຍປາກພາສາລາວ
ບໍ່ໄດ້(ຫລາຍ)

I can't speak Lao well.
khàwy pàak pháa-săa
láo baw keng

ຂ້ອຍປາກພາສາລາວ
ບໍ່ເກັ່ງ

Can you speak English?
jâo pàak pháa-săa ang-kít dâi baw

ເຈົ້າປາກພາສາອັງກິດໄດ້ບໍ່

A little.
náwy neung

ໜ້ອຍໜຶ່ງ

I speak ... [insert country
name from page 50]
khàwy pàak pháa-săa ...

ຂ້ອຍປາກພາສາ ...

Please speak slowly.
ká-lu-náa wâo sâa-sâa

ກະລຸນາເວົ້າຊ້າໆ

Please repeat.
ká-lu-náa wâo khéun mai

ກະລຸນາເວົ້າຄືນໃໝ່

Forgive me, I don't understand.
khăw thôht, khàwy baw khào jai

ຂໍໂທດຂ້ອຍບໍ່ເຂົ້າໃຈ

I/We don't understand.
baw khào jai

ບໍ່ເຂົ້າໃຈ

Do you understand?
jâo khào jai baw

ເຈົ້າເຂົ້າໃຈບໍ່

What?
nyăng

ຫຍັງ

What did you say?
jâo wâo nyăng

ເຈົ້າເວົ້າຫຍັງ

Can you teach me Lao?
jâo săwn pháa-săa láo
hâi khàwy dâi baw

ເຈົ້າສອນພາສາ
ລາວໃຫ້ຂ້ອຍໄດ້ບໍ່

What do you call this in Lao?
an-nîi pháa-săa láo waa nyăng

ອັນນີ້ພາສາລາວວ່າຫຍັງ

NATIONALITIES   ສັນຊາດ

Where do you come from?	jâo máa tae sai	ເຈົ້າມາແຕ່ໃສ
I come from ...	khàwy máa tae ...	ຂ້ອຍມາແຕ່ ...
I'm from ...	khàwy pęn khón ...	ຂ້ອຍເປັນຄົນ ...
Australia	ąw-sá-tąa-líi	ອົສຕາລິ
Canada	kąa-náa-dąa	ການາດາ
China	jiin	ຈິນ
Denmark	dąen-mâak	ແດນມາກ
England	ąng-kít	ອັງກິດ
Europe	yúu-lôhp	ຍູໂລບ
France	fa-lang	ຝະລັ່ງ
Germany	yóe-la-mán	ເຍຍລະມັນ
Holland	háwn-láen	ຮອລແລນ
India	in-dia	ອິນເດຍ
Italy	íi-tąa-líi	ອິຕາລິ
Japan	nyii-pun	ຍີ່ປຸນ
Laos	láo	ລາວ
New Zealand	níu síi-láen	ນິວຊີແລນ
Singapore	sĭng-a-pǫh	ສິງກາໂປ
Spain	sá-pęhn	ສະແປນ
Sweden	sá-wíi-dęn	ສະວິດເດນ
Switzerland	sá-wit-sóe-láen	ສະວິດເຊິແລນ
Taiwan	tâi-wăn	ໄຕ້ຫວັນ
USA	ąa-méh-li-kąa	ອາເມລິກາ

WIT AND WISDOM

You don't need to teach an alligator how to swim.

yaa sąwn khàe láwy nâm   ຢ່າສອນແຂ້ລອຍນ້ຳ

AGE
ອາຍຸ

Asking someone's age is a common question in Laos. It's not considered rude to ask strangers their age.

How old are you?	jâo ạa-nyu ják pịi	ເຈົ້າອາຍຸຈັກປີ
I'm ... years old.	kháwy ạa-nyu ... pịi	ຂ້ອຍອາຍຸ ... ປີ
Very young!	num lǎi	ໜຸ່ມຫລາຍ
Very old!	tháo lǎi	ເຖົ້າຫລາຍ

OCCUPATIONS
ອາຊີບ

I'm a/an ...   khàwy pẹn ...   ຂ້ອຍເປັນ ...

artist	sĭ-la-pịn	ສິລະປິນ
businessperson	nak thu-la-kít	ນັກທຸລະກິດ
diplomat	nak kạan-thûut	ນັກການທູດ
doctor	thaan mǎw	ທ່ານໝໍ
engineer	wit-sáa-wa-kạwn	ວິຊາວະກອນ
farmer	sáo-náa	ຊາວນາ
journalist	nak khao	ນັກຂ່າວ
lawyer	tha-nái-khwáam	ທະນາຍຄວາມ
musician	nak dọn-tịi	ນັກດົນຕີ
policeman	tạm lùat	ຕຳຫລວດ
secretary	léh-khǎa-nu-kạan	ເລຂານຸການ
student	nak séuk-sǎa	ນັກສຶກສາ
teacher	khúu	ຄູ
traveller/tourist	nak thawng thiaw	ນັກທ່ອງທ່ຽວ
volunteer	ạa-sǎa-sá-mak	ອາສາສະມັກ
worker	kạm-ma-kạwn	ກຳມະກອນ

| I'm in the military. | tha-hǎan | ທະຫານ |
| I'm unemployed. | waang ngáan | ຫວ້າງງານ |

FAMILY   ຄອບຄົວ

Laos is a very family-orientated society, so enquiries about one's family are quite common. If you're asked about marriage or children, it's better to respond with the Lao for 'not yet' rather than 'I/We don't want children' or 'I/We have no plans to get married'.

Lao has no specific word for 'cousin'; if you must refer to this relationship, preface the appropriate Lao word for aunt or uncle with lûuk khǎwng ... (ລູກຂອງ ..., 'child of ...').

How many in your family?

   khâwp khúa jǎo míi ják khón   ຄອບຄົວເຈົ້າມີຈັກຄົນ

I have ... in my family.

[for numbers, see page 161]

   míi ... khón   ມີ ... ຄົນ

Are you married (yet)?

   taeng-ngáan lâew léu baw   ແຕ່ງງານແລ້ວຫລືບໍ່

Yes, I'm married.

   taeng-ngáan lâew   ແຕ່ງງານແລ້ວ

I'm not married yet.

   nyáng baw taeng-ngáan   ຍັງບໍ່ແຕ່ງງານ

I'm single.

   pęn sóht   ເປັນໂສດ

Do you have any children (yet)?

   míi lûuk lâew baw   ມີລູກແລ້ວບໍ່

I have ... child/children.

   míi lûuk ... khón lâew   ມີລູກ ... ຄົນແລ້ວ

I don't have children yet.

   nyáng baw míi lûuk   ຍັງບໍ່ມີລູກ

Family Members

สะมาชิกถอบถัอ

aunt (older sister of either parent)	pâa	ป้า
child/children	lûuk	ลูก
daughter	lûuk sǎo	ลูกสาว
family	khâwp khúa	ถอบถัว
father	phaw	พ่
father's side		
grandfather	púu	ปู่
grandmother	yaa	ย่า
aunt	ąa	อา
uncle	ao	อาว
husband	phǔa	ผิว
mother	mae	แม่
mother's side		
grandfather	phaw thào	พ่เฒ็า
grandmother	mae thào	แม่เฒ็า
aunt	nâa	ป้า
uncle	nâa bao	ป้าบ่าว
niece/nephew	lǎan	ຫລາມ
older sister	êuay	เอื้อย
older brother	âai	อ้าย
parents	phaw-mae	พ่แม่
relatives	phii-nâwng	พิมอง
son	lûuk sáai	ลูกชาย
uncle (older brother of either parent)	lúng	ลุง
wife	mía	เมย
younger sister	nâwng sǎo	มองสาว
younger brother	nâwng sáai	มองชาย
younger sibling	náwng	มอง

THE POWER BEHIND THE ELEPHANT

Lao women have substantial gender parity in the workforce, inheritance, land ownership and so on, often more so than in many Western countries. The bad news is that, although women generally fare well in these areas, their cultural standing is a bit further from parity. An oft-repeated Lao saying reminds us that men form the front legs of the elephant, women the hind legs.

Lao Buddhism commonly holds that women must be reborn as men before they can attain nirvana, though many *dhamma* teachers point out that this presumption isn't supported by the suttas (discourses of the Buddha) or by the commentaries. But nevertheless it is a widespread belief.

While many Lao taboos can be bent a little without creating a huge fuss, the following one cannot. Aboard transport such as trucks, buses or riverboats in Laos, women are expected to ride inside. Any attempt to ride on the roof will be immediately discouraged. When asked why women can't sit on the roof, the usual Lao answer is phít sàat-sá-náa – 'it's against the religion', which is to say it's against Lao custom. Partially this is old-fashioned chivalry – 'it's too dangerous on the roof' – but mainly it's due to a deep-seated superstition that women's bodies should not intentionally occupy a physical space above a man's for fear of damaging men's spiritual status. Men wearing sacred tattoos or amulets often express the fear that such an arrangement will ruin the protection that these symbols are supposed to convey! The superstition runs to how laundry is hung out to dry. Women's clothing – especially underwear – is not to be hung above men's clothing.

FEELINGS ການສະແດງຄວາມຮູ້ສຶກ

The Lao are much less apt to express their feelings or emotions to strangers than most Western nationalities. Use discretion – any display or expression of strong emotion means a potential loss of face for both speaker and listener.

I feel ...	khàwy hûu-séuk ...	ຂ້ອຍຮູ້ສຶກ ...
angry	jai hâai	ໃຈຮ້າຍ
excited	teun tên	ຕື່ນເຕັ້ນ
happy	dii jai	ດີໃຈ
lonely	ngǎo	ເຫງົາ
nervous (anxious)	ká-wón ká-wáai	ກະວົນກະວາຍ
proud	phúum jai	ພູມໃຈ
sad	sâo sòhk	ເສົ້າໂສກ
satisfied	pháw jai	ພໍໃຈ
sleepy	nguang náwn	ງ່ວງນອນ
surprised	pá-láat jai	ປະຫລາດໃຈ
tired	meuay	ເມື່ອຍ
upset	ạa-lóm sǐa	ອາລົມເສຍ

I'm bored.	beua	ເບື່ອ
This is fun!	muan dii	ມ່ວນດີ

OPINIONS ການອອກຄຳເຫັນ

I feel that ...	khàwy hûu-séuk waa ...	ຂ້ອຍຮູ້ສຶກວ່າ ...
I think that ...	khàwy khit waa ...	ຂ້ອຍຄິດວ່າ ...
I agree.	khàwy hěn dii	ຂ້ອຍເຫັນດີ
I disagree.	baw hěn dii	ບໍ່ເຫັນດີ
In my opinion ...	khwáam khit khàwng khàwy ...	ຄວາມຄິດຂອງ ຂ້ອຍ ...
As for me ...	sǎm-láp khàwy ...	ສຳລັບຂ້ອຍ ...
It's not important.	baw sǎm-khán	ບໍ່ສຳຄັນ

MEETING PEOPLE

COMMON INTERESTS ຄວາມສົນໃຈທົ່ວໄປ

What do you do in your spare time?

	nái wéh-láah wàang jâo	ໃນເວລາຫວ້າງ
	het nyǎng	ເຈົ້າເຮັດຫຍັງ

I like ...	khàwy mak ...	ຂ້ອຍມັກ ...
I don't like ...	khàwy baw mak ...	ຂ້ອຍບໍ່ມັກ ...
Do you like ...?	jâo mak ... baw	ເຈົ້າມັກ ... ບໍ່
art	sí-la-pá	ສິລະປະ
cooking	taeng kịn	ແຕ່ງກິນ
dancing	fâwn	ຟ້ອນ
film	nǎng leuang	ໜັງເລື່ອງ
going out	àwk pại tháang nâwk	ອອກໄປທາງນອກ
music	dọn-tjii	ດົນຕີ
photography	thaai hûup	ຖ່າຍຮູບ
playing games	lìn kẹhm	ຫລິ້ນເກມ
playing soccer	lìn bạan-té	ຫລິ້ນບານເຕະ
playing sport	lìn kí-láa	ຫລິ້ນກິລາ
reading books	aan pêum	ອ່ານປຶ້ມ
shopping	pại sêu kheuang	ໄປຊື້ເຄື່ອງ
the theatre	boeng la-kháwn	ເບິ່ງລະຄອນ
travelling	thawng thiaw	ທ່ອງທ່ຽວ
watching TV	boeng thóh-la-that	ເບິ່ງໂທລະທັດ
writing	khǐan	ຂຽນ

SPORT

ກິລາ

Do you like sport?
jâo mak lìn kí-láa baw

ເຈົ້າມັກຫລິ້ນກິລາບໍ່

I like playing sport.
mak lìn kí-láa

ມັກຫລິ້ນກິລາ

I prefer to watch rather
than play sport.
mak boeng lǎai kwaa lìn

ມັກເບິ່ງຫລາຍກ່ວາຫລິ້ນ

Do you play ...?
jâo lìn baw ...

ເຈົ້າຫລິ້ນບໍ່ ...

Would you like to play ...?
jâo yàak lìn ... baw

ເຈົ້າຢາກຫລິ້ນ ... ບໍ່

HEAD OVER HEELS

Ká-tâw (ກະຕໍ້), a contest in which a woven rattan – or
sometimes plastic – ball approximately 12cm in diameter
is kicked around, is almost as popular in Laos as it is in
Thailand and Malaysia.

The traditional way to play ká-tâw is for players to stand
in a circle (the size of the circle depends on the number of
players) and simply try to keep the ball airborne by kicking
it soccer-style. Points are scored for style, difficulty and
variety of kicking manoeuvres.

A popular variation on ká-tâw – and the one used in
local or international competitions – is played with a
volleyball net, using all the same rules as in volleyball
except that only the feet and head are permitted to touch
the ball. It's amazing to see the players perform aerial
pirouettes, spiking the ball over the net with their feet.

baseball	bẹhs-bạwn	ເບສບອມ
basketball	bạan bâwng	ບາມບ້ອງ
boxing	tịi múay	ຕີມວຍ
diving	dạm nám	ດຳນ້ຳ
gymnastics	kịm-náa-sa-tík	ກິມນນາສຕິກ
hockey	tịi-khíi thóeng nâm kâwn	ຕີຕີເຫ້ິງນ້ຳຫ້ອນ
keeping fit	hak-sǎa sú-khá-phâap	ຮັກສາສຸຂະພາບ
martial arts	kạan sok múay	ການຊົກມວຍ
rugby	lak-bịi	ລັກບີ
skiing	lìn sá-kịi	ຫລິ້ນສະກີ
soccer (football)	bạan-té	ບາມເຕະ
swimming	láwy nâm	ລອຍບ້ຳ
takraw	ká-tâw	ກະຕ້
tennis	tẹn-nîit	ເຕັມບິສ

FINDING YOUR WAY   ການຊອກທິດທາງ

Street signs in cities and towns in Laos are mostly written in Lao script only, although signs at major intersections in Vientiane are also written in French. The French designations for street names vary (eg, route, rue and avenue), but the Lao script always reads tha-nǒn (ຖະໜົນ), which means the same as all the French and English variations. Therefore, when asking directions it's always best to avoid possible confusion and use the Lao word tha-nǒn.

Excuse me, can you help me?		ຂໍໂທດ ຊ່ວຍຂ້ອຍໄດ້ບໍ່
khǎw thôht,		
suay khàwy dâi baw		

Where's the ...?	... yùu sǎi	...ຢູ່ໃສ
bus station	sá-thǎa-níi lot	ສະຖານີລົດ
	pá-jạm tháang	ປະຈຳທາງ
bus stop	bawn jàwt lot	ບ່ອນຈອດລົດ
	pá-jạm tháang	ປະຈຳທາງ
taxi stand	bawn jàwt lot	ບ່ອນຈອດລົດ
	thaek-sîi	ແທັກຊີ

Which ...	bawn nîi maen	ບ່ອນນີ້ແມ່ນ
is this?	... nyǎng	...ຫຍັງ
avenue/street/road	tha-nǒn	ຖະໜົນ
city	méuang	ເມືອງ
province	khwǎeng	ແຂວງ
village	muu bâan	ໝູ່ບ້ານ

I want to go to ...	khàwy yàak pại ...	ຂ້ອຍຢາກໄປ ...
I'm looking for ...	khàwy sâwk hǎa ...	ຂ້ອຍຊອກຫາ ...

GETTING AROUND

What time will the ... leave?	... já àwk ják móhng	... ຈະອອກຈັກ ໂມງ
aeroplane	héua bin	ເຮືອບິນ
boat	héua	ເຮືອ
minivan	lot tûu	ລົດຕູ້

DIRECTIONS   ທິດທາງ

Excuse me, I'm looking for ...
khăw thôht, khàwy sâwk hăa ...   ຂໍໂທດ ຂ້ອຍຊອກຫາ ...
How many kilometres from here?
jàak nîi pại ják kí-lóh-maet   ຈາກນີ້ໄປຈັກກີໂລແມັດ

Turn ...	lîaw ...	ລ້ຽວ ...
left	sâai	ຊ້າຍ
right	khwăa	ຂວາ

Go straight ahead.	pại seu-seu	ໄປຊື່ໆ
Turn around.	lîaw káp	ລ້ຽວກັບ
Turn back.	káp máa	ກັບມາ
How far?	kại thao dại	ໄກເທົ່າໃດ

| (not) far | (baw) kại | (ບໍ່) ໄກ |
| (not) near | (baw) kâi | (ບໍ່) ບໍ່ໄກ |

north	thit nĕua	ທິດເໜືອ
south	thit tâi	ທິດໃຕ້
east	thit tạa-wén àwk	ທິດຕາເວັນອອກ
west	thit tạa-wén tók	ທິດຕາເວັນຕົກ

STREET TALK

Street addresses are rarely used in Laos outside of Vientiane. Even in the capital city, jumbo drivers may be unable to locate a specific street address, since the numbering of buildings – both residential and commercial – tends to follow the order of construction, not the position of a building on a street.

Tha-nǒn (ถะໜົນ) is the general all-purpose Lao word meaning street, road, avenue and so on. A typical street address – where they exist – might be 69 Thanon Lan Xang. Outside of the central Chanthabuli méuang (ເມືອງ, roughly, 'district') of Vientiane, few streets in Laos have signs bearing the name of the street. When such signs do exist, they are usually in Lao script only.

The méuang of Vientiane are broken up into bâan (ບ້ານ), which are neighbourhoods or villages associated with local wats. Wattay International Airport, for example, is in Ban Wat Tai, a village in the southern part of Muang Sikhottabong centred around Wat Tai.

BUYING TICKETS ການຊື້ແລະການຈອງປີ້

I would like a ticket.		
khàwy yàak dâi pîi		ຂ້ອຍຢາກໄດ້ປີ້
I would like two tickets.		
khàwy yàak dâi pîi sǎwng bại		ຂ້ອຍຢາກໄດ້ປີ້ສອງໃບ
Are there any tickets to ...?		
mii pîi pại ...		ມີປີ້ໄປ ...
How much per place (seat, deck space, etc)?		
bawn-la thao dại		ບ່ອນລະເທົ່າໃດ
How many departures are there ...?	... mii ják thîaw	... ມີຈັກທ່ຽວ
today	mêu nîi	ມື້ນີ້
tomorrow	mêu eun	ມື້ອື່ນ

GETTING AROUND

We would like to reserve ... places.
phûak háo yàak jawng   ພວກເຮົາຢາກ
bawn ... bawn   ຈອງບ່ອນ ... ບ່ອນ
I'd like to change my ticket.
khàwy yàak pian pîi   ຂ້ອຍຢາກປ່ຽນປີ້
I'd like a refund on my ticket.
khàwy yàak khéun pîi   ຂ້ອຍຢາກຄືນປີ້
I'm sorry, I've changed my mind.
khǎw thôht, khàwy pian   ຂໍໂທດ ຂ້ອຍປ່ຽນໃຈແລ້ວ
jai lâew

AIR   ທາງອາກາດ

Lao Aviation handles all domestic flights in Laos. You can purchase
domestic tickets and make reservations at airline offices or travel
agencies in every city that has an airfield.

aeroplane	héua bịn; nyón	ເຮືອບິນ; ຍົນ
airlines	kạan-bịn	ການບິນ
airport	doen bịn	ເດີ່ນບິນ
departures/flights	thîaw bịn	ຖ້ຽວບິນ
Lao Aviation	kạan-bịn láo	ການບິນລາວ
plane tickets	pîi héua bịn; pîi nyón	ປີ້ເຮືອບິນ; ປີ້ຍົນ

Is there a flight to ...?
míi thîaw bịn pại ...   ມີຖ້ຽວບິນໄປ ...
When's the next flight to ...?
wéh-láa dại míi thîaw   ເວລາໃດມີຖ້ຽວບິນຕໍ່ໄປ ...
bịn taw pại ...
What time will the plane leave?
héua bịn si khèun ják móhng   ເຮືອບິນຊິຂຶ້ນຈັກໂມງ
How long does the flight take?
sâi wéh-láa bịn dọn pạan dại ໃຊ້ເວລາບິນດົນປານໃດ

BUS
ລົດເມ

Where roads are surfaced, buses are an inexpensive and very acceptable way to get from one point to another. Outside the Mekong River Valley, Soviet, Vietnamese or Japanese trucks are often converted into passenger carriers by adding two long benches in the back. These passenger trucks are called tháek-síi (ແທັກຊີ້, taxis), or in some areas săwng-thăew (ສອງແຖວ, songthaew), which means 'two rows', in reference to the benches in the back.

Where public bus service isn't available, the Lao often travel long road distances by arranging rides with trucks carrying cargo from one province to another.

bus station	sá-thăa-níi lot pá-jạm tháang (khíu lot méh)	ສະຖານີລົດປະຈຳທາງ (ຄິວລົດເມ)
Which bus goes to ...?	lot khán dại pai ...	ລົດຄັນໃດໄປ ...
Does this bus go to ...?	lot khán níi pai ... baw	ລົດຄັນນີ້ໄປ ... ບໍ່
How many departures are there today/tomorrow?	mêu-níi/mêu-eun míi ják thîaw	ມື້ນີ້/ມື້ອື່ນ ມີຈັກຖ້ຽວ
What time will the bus leave?	lot já àwk ják móhng	ລົດຈະອອກຈັກໂມງ

What time's the ... bus?	lot ... àwk ják móhng	ລົດ ... ອອກຈັກໂມງ
first	khán thii neung	ຄັນທີໜຶ່ງ
last	khán sut-thâai	ຄັນສຸດທ້າຍ
next	khán taw pại	ຄັນຕໍ່ໄປ

Could you tell me when we get to ...?	jáo suay bàwk khàwy dâi baw wéh-láa pại hâwt ...	ເຈົ້າຊ່ວຍບອກຂ້ອຍໄດ້ບໍ່ ເວລາໄປຮອດ ...
I want to get off.	khàwy yàak lóng	ຂ້ອຍຢາກລົງ

GETTING AROUND

TAXI   ແທັກຊຸ

Each of the country's three largest towns – Vientiane, Luang Prabang and Savannakhet – has a handful of car taxis that are used by foreign businesspeople and the occasional tourist. The only place you'll find these taxis is at the airports (arrival times only) and in front of the larger hotels. Taxis like these can be hired by the trip, by the hour or by the day.

taxi   lot thâek-síi   ລົດແທັກຊີ່

SAMLORS & JUMBOS   ສາມລໍ້ແລະຈຳໂບ້

Once a mainstay of local transport throughout urban Laos, the bicycle samlor has all but disappeared. When you can find them, samlor fares cost about the same as motorcycle taxis but are generally used only for distances less than 2km or so.

Three-wheeled motorcycle taxis are common in large cities. This type of vehicle can be called thâek-síi (ແທັກຊີ່, taxi) or sǎam-lâw (ສາມລໍ້, 'three-wheels'). The larger ones made in Thailand are called jam-bọh (ຈຳໂບ້, 'jumbos') and can hold four to six passengers. In Vientiane they are also sometimes called túk-túk (ຕຸກໆ) as in Thailand, while in the south (Pakse, Savannakhet) they may be called 'Skylab' because of the perceived resemblance to a space capsule! They can go anywhere a regular taxi can go, but aren't usually hired for distances greater than 20km or so.

jumbo   jam-bọh   ຈຳໂບ້
samlor (pedicab)   sǎam-lâw   ສາມລໍ້

How much to ...?
   pại ... thao dại ໄປ ... ເທົ່າໃດ

Too expensive. How about ... kìp?
   pháeng phôht. ... kíp dâi baw ແພງໂພດ ... ກີບໄດ້ບໍ່

Agreed. Let's go.
   tók-lóng. lâew pại ຕົກລົງ ແລ້ວໄປ

Drive slowly please.
   ká-lu-náa kháp sâa-sâa dae ກະລຸນາຂັບຊ້າໆແດ່

Continue!
   kháp taw pại iik ຂັບຕໍ່ໄປອີກ

Take the next street to the left/right.
   hâwt tháang taw pại lâew ຣອດທາງຕໍ່ໄປແລ້ວ
   lîaw sâai/khwǎa ລ້ຽວຊ້າຍ/ຂວາ

Please wait here.
   ká-lu-náa thàa yuu nîi ກະລຸນາຖ້າຢູ່ນີ້

Stop at the corner.
   ká-lu-náa jàwt yuu múum nîi ກະລຸນາຈອດຢູ່ມູມນີ້

Stop here.
   jàwt yuu nîi ຈອດຢູ່ນີ້

OUT FOR A TEN COUNT

1	neung	ໜຶ່ງ
2	sǎwng	ສອງ
3	sǎam	ສາມ
4	sii	ສີ່
5	hàa	ຫ້າ
6	hók	ຫົກ
7	jét	ເຈັດ
8	pàet	ແປດ
9	kâo	ເກົ້າ
10	síp	ສິບ

GETTING AROUND

BOAT

เรือ

Rivers are the traditional highways and byways of Laos, the main thoroughfares being the Mekong, Nam Ou, Nam Khan, Nam Tha, Nam Ngum and Se Don. The Mekong is the longest and most important water route and is navigable year-round between Luang Prabang in the north and Don Khong in the south.

For long distances, large diesel river ferries with overnight accommodation are used. For shorter river trips (eg, from Luang Prabang to the Pak Ou caves), it's usually best to hire a river taxi, since the large river ferries only ply their routes a couple of times a week. The longtail boats, with engines gimbal-mounted on the stern, are the most typical, though for a really short trip, such as crossing a river, a rowboat can be hired.

Along the upper Mekong River between Luang Prabang and Huay Sai, Thai-built speedboats – shallow, five-metre-long skiffs with 40-hp outboard engines – are common.

boat	héua	เรือ
boat taxi	héua jàang	เรือจ้าง
cross-river ferry	héua khàam fâak;	เรือข้ามฟาก/
	héua bák	เรือบัก
longtail boat	héua hǎang nyáo	เรือหางยาว
row boat	héua phái	เรือพาย
speed boat	héua wái	เรือไว

Where do we get on the boat?
    lóng héua yuu sǎi
    ลงเรืออยู่ใส

What time does the boat leave?
    héua já àwk ják móhng
    เรือจะออกจักโມງ

What time does the boat arrive?
    héua já máa hâwt ják móhng
    เรือจะมารอดจักโມງ

USEFUL WORDS & PHRASES

ຄຳສັບແລະປະໂຫຍກທີ່
ເປັນປະໂຫຍດ

arrive	máa hâwt	ມາຮອດ
bridge	khǔa	ຂົວ
charter vehicle	lot jàang	ລົດຈ້າງ
daily	pá-jam mêu (thuk mêu)	ປະຈຳມື້ (ທຸກມື້)
detour	tháang wêhn	ທາງເວັ້ນ
drive	kháp	ຂັບ
early	sâo	ເຊົ້າ
fast	wái	ໄວ
hire/charter	jàang	ຈ້າງ
leave	àwk	ອອກ
pier	thaa héua	ທ່າເຮືອ
'regular vehicle' (ie, not a charter vehicle)	lot pá-jam	ລົດປະຈຳ
seat	bawn nang	ບ່ອນນັ່ງ
slow	sâa	ຊ້າ
stop/park	jàwt	ຈອດ

What time does it leave here?
    já àwk jàak nîi ják móhng   ຈະອອກຈາກນີ້ຈັກໂມງ

What time does it arrive there?
    já pai hâwt phún ják móhng   ຈະໄປຮອດພຸ້ນຈັກໂມງ

What time does the first vehicle leave?
    khán thii neung já àwk
    ják móhng   ຄັນທີ່ນຶ່ງຈະອອກຈັກໂມງ

What time does the last vehicle leave?
    khán sút-thâai já àwk
    ják móhng   ຄັນສຸດທ້າຍຈະອອກ
    ຈັກໂມງ

What's the fare?
  khaa dǫen tháang thao dại   ຄ່າເດີນທາງເທົ່າໃດ

How much per person?
  khón-la thao dại   ຄົນລະເທົ່າໃດ

I/We don't want to charter
a vehicle.
  baw yàak jàang lot   ບໍ່ຍາກຈ້າງລົດ

I/We want to charter a vehicle.
  yàak jàang lot   ຍາກຈ້າງລົດ

Can you lower the price?
  lut láa-kháa dâi baw   ລຸດລາຄາໄດ້ບໍ່

Can you lower (the price) more?
  lut ìik dâi baw   ລຸດອິກໄດ້ບໍ່

Where does the vehicle
depart from?
  lot àwk yuu sǎi   ລົດອອກຢູ່ໃສ

Where can we get on the vehicle?
  khèun lot yuu sǎi   ຂຶ້ນລົດຢູ່ໃສ

Is there anyone sitting here?
  mii phǎi nang yuu nîi baw   ມີໃຜນັ່ງຢູ່ນີ້ບໍ່

May I sit here?
  nang bawn nîi dâi baw   ນັ່ງບ່ອນນີ້ໄດ້ບໍ່

Can I put my bag here?
  wáang thǒng yuu nîi dâi baw   ວາງຖົງຢູ່ນີ້ໄດ້ບໍ່

Can you wait for me?
  thàa khàwy dâi baw   ຖ້າຂ້ອຍໄດ້ບໍ່

Can you wait here?
  jâo thàa yuu nîi dâi baw ··· ເຈົ້າຖ້າຍູ່ນີ້ໄດ້ບໍ່

Where are you going?
  pai sǎi ··· ໄປໃສ

I want to go to ...
  khàwy yàak pai ... ··· ຂ້ອຍຢາກໄປ ...

I'll get out here.
  khàwy si long bawn nîi ··· ຂ້ອຍຊິລົງບ່ອນນີ້

Which vehicle goes to ...?
  lot khan dại pai ... ··· ລົດຄັນໃດໄປ ...

When we arrive in ...,
please tell me.
  wéh-láa hâwt ... ··· ເວລາຮອດ ...
  bàwk khàwy dae ··· ບອກຂ້ອຍແດ່

Can we stop over in ...?
  long phak yuu ... dâi baw ··· ລົງພັກຍູ່ ... ໄດ້ບໍ່

Stop here.
  jàwt bawn nîi ··· ຈອດບ່ອນນີ້

RENTING VEHICLES

ການເຊົ່າລົດ,
ລົດຈັກແລະລົດຖີບ

Cars, motorcycles and bicycles can be rented in Vientiane and to a lesser degree in Luang Prabang. Bicycles can usually be arranged in smaller towns and are a good way of getting around since traffic is relatively light.

I'd like to rent a ...	khàwy yàak sao ...	ຂ້ອຍຢາກເຊົ່າ ...
bicycle	lot thìip	ລົດຖີບ
car	lot oh-tọh	ລົດໂອໂຕ
motorcycle	lot ják	ລົດຈັກ
truck	lot bạn-thuk	ລົດບັນທຸກ

GETTING AROUND

How much per/for ...?	... thao dại	... ເທົ່າໃດ
hour	sua-móhng-la	ຊົ່ວໂມງລະ
day	mêu-la	ມື້ລະ
week	ąa-thit-la	ອາທິດລະ
month	dẹuan-la	ເດືອນລະ
three days	săam mêu	ສາມມື້

Does the price include insurance?
láa-kháa huam nám
pá-kạn phái baw

ລາຄາຮ່ວມນຳປະກັນໄພບໍ່

Where's the next petrol station?
pâm nâm-mán taw
pại yuu săi

ປໍ້ນ້ຳມັນຕໍ່ໄປຢູ່ໃສ

WAVING THE FLAG

Laos' national seal, often applied to official government publications, features a near-complete circle formed by curving rice stalks which enclose six component symbols of the productive proletarian state: Vientiane's Pha That Luang (representing religion); a checkerboard of rice fields (agriculture); gear cogs (industry); a dam (energy); a highway (transport); and a grove of trees (forestry). A label in Lao script at the bottom of the seal reads 'Lao People's Democratic Republic'.

The national flag consists of two horizontal bars of red (symbolising courage and heroism), above and below a bar of blue (nationhood) on which is centred a blank white sphere (the light of communism), sometimes also interpreted as a moon. This flag is flown in front of all government offices and by some private citizens on National Day (2 December). On this holiday the Lao national flag may be joined by a second flag featuring a yellow hammer and sickle centred on a field of red, the international symbol of communism.

Please fill the tank.
   ká-lu-náa sai nâm-man   ກະລຸນາໃສ່
   hài tem thăng   ນ້ຳມັນໃຫ້ເຕັມຖັງ

I'd like ... litres.
   sai ... lit   ໃສ່ ...ລິດ

Does this road lead to ...?
   tháang nîi pai hâwt ... baw   ທາງນີ້ໄປຮອດ ... ບໍ່

Please check the ...	ká-lu-náa kùat ...	ກະລຸນາກວດ ...
air	lóm	ລົມ
oil	nâm-mán	ນ້ຳມັນ
water	nâm	ນ້ຳ
tyre pressure	khwáam dạn	ຄວາມດັນ
	khǎwng yáang lot	ຂອງຢາງລົດ

CAR PROBLEMS   ບັນຫາລົດ

We need a mechanic.
   phûak háo tâwng-kạan   ພວກເຮົາຕ້ອງການ
   saang pạeng ják   ຊ່າງແປງຈັກ

What make is it?
   yii hàw nyǎng   ຍີ່ຫໍ້ຫຍັງ

Can you repair it?
   jâo pạeng dâi baw   ເຈົ້າແປງໄດ້ບໍ່

The battery's flat.
   màw fái awn   ໝໍ້ໄຟອ່ອນ

I have a flat tyre.
   yáang lot khàwy sìa   ຢາງລົດຂ້ອຍຊື່ວ

It's overheating.
   mán hâwn lǎai phôht   ມັນຮ້ອນຫລາຍໂພດ

The radiator's leaking.
   màw nâm hua   ໝໍ້ນ້ຳຮົ່ວ

It's not working.
   mán baw het wîak   ມັນບໍ່ເຮັດວຽກ

GETTING AROUND

Useful Words

ສັບທີ່ເປັນປະໂຫຍດ

battery	màw fái	ໝໍ້ໄຟ
brakes	hàam	ຫ້າມ
clutch	khâat	ຄາດ
drivers licence	bại á-nu-nyâat kháp khii	ໃບອະນຸຍາດຂັບຂີ່
engine	kheuang ják	ເຄື່ອງຈັກ
garage	uu sàwm pạeng lot	ອູ່ສ້ອມແປງລົດ
headlight	fái tạa tháang nàa	ໄຟຕາທາງໜ້າ
insurance	pá-kạn phái	ປະກັນໄພ
lights	fái	ໄຟ
mechanic	saang pạeng ják	ຊ່າງແປງຈັກ
motor oil	nâm-mán kheuang	ນ້ຳມັນເຄື່ອງ
oil	nâm-mán	ນ້ຳມັນ
petrol (gasoline)	nâm-mán (áet-sáng)	ນ້ຳມັນ (ແອັດຊັງ)
petrol station	pâm nâm-mán	ປັ້ມນ້ຳມັນ
puncture	hua/jáw	ຮົ່ວ/ເຈາະ
radiator	màw nâm	ໝໍ້ນ້ຳ
tyre	yạang lot	ຍາງລົດ
wheel	lâw	ລໍ້
windscreen	waen nàa	ແຫວ່ນໜ້າ

ສະຖານ ທີ່ພັກແຮມ ACCOMMODATION

In Laos, generally speaking, a 'single' means a room with one large bed that will sleep two, while a 'double' has two large beds. Room rates are thus quoted according to the number of beds a room has, rather than the number of guests who will be using the room. This is especially true for guesthouses. On the other hand, a few larger, Western-style hotels do calculate room tariffs according to the number of guests per room.

An 'ordinary room' (ຫ້ອງທໍາມະດາ, hàwng thám-ma-daa) usually means a less expensive room with a fan rather than with air-conditioning.

If you find yourself in a town or village where no hotels or guesthouses are available, or where they are all full, you may be invited to stay with local residents. In such cases you may be asked for a small fee. If not, it's good form to offer a gift – preferably food or something needed in the household – to your hosts.

FINDING ACCOMMODATION
ການຊອກ ສະຖານທີ່ພັກແຮມ

hotel	hóhng háem	ໂຮງແຮມ
guesthouse	héuan phak	ເຮືອນພັກ

Excuse me, is there a hotel nearby?
khǎw thôht, míi hóhng
háem yuu kâi níi baw
ຂໍໂທດ ມີໂຮງແຮມ
ຢູ່ໃກ້ນີ້ບໍ່

Is this a hotel?
níi maen hóhng háem baw
ນີ້ແມ່ນໂຮງແຮມບໍ່

Is this a guesthouse?
níi maen héuan phak baw
ນີ້ແມ່ນເຮືອນພັກບໍ່

Is there a place to stay here?
yuu níi míi bawn phak baw
ຢູ່ນີ້ມີບ່ອນພັກບໍ່

73

ACCOMMODATION

We need a place to stay.
  phûak háo tâwng-kạan   ພວກເຮົາຕ້ອງການ
  bawn phak   ບ່ອນພັກ
Can I/we stay here?
  phak yuu nîi dâi baw   ພັກຢູ່ນີ້ໄດ້ບໍ່
Can I/we sleep here?
  náwn yuu nîi dâi baw   ນອນຢູ່ນີ້ໄດ້ບໍ່

CHECKING IN   ການແຈ້ງເຂົ້າ

air-conditioning	ạe yẹn	ແອເຢັນ
bathroom	hàwng nâm	ຫ້ອງນ້ຳ
double room	hàwng náwn tịang khuu	ຫ້ອງນອນຕຽງຄູ່
fan	phat lóm	ພັດລົມ
hot water	nâm hâwn	ນ້ຳຮ້ອນ
not vacant	baw waang	ບໍ່ຫວ້າງ
room	hàwng	ຫ້ອງ
single room	hàwng náwn tịang diaw	ຫ້ອງນອນຕຽງດ່ຽວ
toilet	sùam	ສ້ວມ
vacant	waang	ຫວ້າງ

Do you have a room?
  míi hàwng baw   ມີຫ້ອງບໍ່
How many people?
  ják khón   ຈັກຄົນ

one person   neung khón; khón diaw   ໜຶ່ງຄົນ; ຄົນດ່ຽວ
two people   sǎwng khón   ສອງຄົນ

How much per/for ...?	... thao dại	... ເທົ່າໃດ
night	khéun-la	ຄືນລະ
week	ạa-thit-la	ອາທິດລະ
month	dèuan-la	ເດືອນລະ
three nights	sǎam khéun	ສາມຄືນ

It's too expensive.
pháeng phôht   ແພງໂພດ

I/We will stay two nights.
síi phak sǎwng khéun   ຊີພັກສອງຄືນ

Can you lower the price?
lut láa-kháa dâi baw   ລຸດລາຄາໄດ້ບໍ່

Can I/we look at the room?
khaw beong hàwng dâi baw   ຂໍເບິ່ງຫ້ອງໄດ້ບໍ່

Do you have any other rooms?
míi hàwng eun íik baw   ມີຫ້ອງອື່ນອີກບໍ່

I/We want an ordinary room.
ạo hàwng thám-ma-dạa   ເອົາຫ້ອງທຳມະດາ

We need a ...	phûak háo tâwng-kạan	ພວກເຮົາ
room than this.	hàwng ... nîi	ຕ້ອງການຫ້ອງ ... ນີ້
cheaper	théuk-kwaa	ຖຶກກວ່າ
larger	nyai-kwaa	ໃຫຍ່ກວ່າ
smaller	nâwy-kwaa	ນ້ອຍກວ່າ
quieter	mit-kwaa	ມິດກວ່າ

ACCOMMODATION

WIT & WISDOM

It's easy to earn money but difficult to find kindness.

ngóen khám hǎa dâi,   ເງິນຄຳຫາໄດ້
nâm jại hǎa yàak   ນ້ຳໃຈຫາຍາກ

ACCOMMODATION

REQUESTS & COMPLAINTS

ການຮ້ອງຂໍ ແລະຕໍ່ວ່າ

Is there ...?	míi ... baw	ມີ ... ບໍ່
a telephone	thóh-la-sáp	ໂທລະສັບ
hot water	nâm hâwn	ນ້ຳຮ້ອນ

I/We need (a) ...	tâwng-kaan ...	ຕ້ອງການ ...
another bed	tiang ìik	ຕຽງອີກ
blanket	phàa hom	ຜ້າຫົ່ມ
key	ká-jae	ກະແຈ
pillow	mǎwn	ໝອນ
sheet	phàa puu bawn	ຜ້າປູບ່ອນ
soap	sá-buu	ສະບູ
towel	phàa set toh	ຜ້າເຊັດໂຕ

Can you clean the room?
    á-náa-mái hàwng   ອະນາໄມຫ້ອງໃຫ້ແດ່ໄດ້ບໍ່
    hài dae dâi baw

This room isn't clean.
    hàwng nîi baw sá-àat   ຫ້ອງນີ້ບໍ່ສະອາດ

There's no hot water.
    baw míi nâm hâwn   ບໍ່ມີນ້ຳຮ້ອນ

Can you repair it?
    jâo paeng hài dae dâi baw   ເຈົ້າແປງໃຫ້ແດ່ໄດ້ບໍ່

CHECKING OUT

ການແຈ້ງອອກ

bill	bai bin	ໃບບິນ
receipt	bai hap ngóen	ໃບຮັບເງິນ
service charge	khaa baw-li-kaan	ຄ່າບໍລິການ
tax	pháa-sǐi	ພາສີ

I/We will return in two weeks.
    ìik sǎwng aa-thit síi káp máa   ອີກສອງອາທິດຊິກັບມາ

Can I store my bags here?
    fàak kheuang yuu nîi dâi baw   ຝາກເຄື່ອງຢູ່ນີ້ໄດ້ບໍ່

LAUNDRY   ຊັກເຄື່ອງ

Can you wash these clothes?
    sak séua phàa nîi dâi baw   ຊັກເສື້ອຜ້ານີ້ໄດ້ບໍ່

Where can I wash my
clothes (myself)?
    khàwy sak séua phàa   ຂ້ອຍຊັກເສື້ອຜ້າ
    ęhng dâi yuu sǎi   ເອງໄດ້ຢູ່ໃສ

Is there a laundry near here?
    yuu thǎew nîi míi bawn   ຢູ່ແຖວນີ້ມີບ່ອນ
    sak lîit baw   ຊັກລີດບໍ່

No starch.
    baw lóng pâeng   ບໍ່ລົງແປ້ງ

Add starch.
    lóng pâeng   ລົງແປ້ງ

These clothes aren't very clean.
    séua phàa nîi baw   ເສື້ອຜ້ານີ້ບໍ່ສະອາດເທົ່າໃດ
    sá-áat thao dại

Please wash them again.
    ká-lu-náa sak íik theua   ກະລຸນາຊັກອີກເທື່ອ

dry-clean	sak háeng	ຊັກແຫ້ງ
iron (n)	tạo lîit	ເຕົາລິດ
to iron	lîit	ລິດ
laundry service	bạw-li-kạan sak lîit	ບໍລິການຊັກລິດ

ACCOMMODATION

YES, NO, MAYBE...

'Yes' and 'No' don't exist in Lao in the same way as
in English – it depends on the verb used in the
question. Refer to page 42 for the basics on
answering questions.

ACCOMMODATION

Useful Words   ຄຳສັບທີ່ເປັນປະໂຫຍດ

accommodation	bawn phak	ບ່ອນພັກ
to bathe	áap nâm	ອາບນ້ຳ
bathroom	tjang náwn	ຕຽງນອນ
bedroom	hàwng náwn	ຫ້ອງນອນ
breakfast	ąa-hǎan sáo	ອາຫານເຊົ້າ
electricity	fái fàa	ໄຟຟ້າ
elevator (lift)	lip	ລິບ
entrance	tháang khào	ທາງເຂົ້າ
exit	tháang àwk	ທາງອອກ
fan	phat lóm	ພັດລົມ
food	ąa-hǎan	ອາຫານ
lights	fái	ໄຟ

LOOKING FOR ...   ກຳລັງຊອກຫາ ...

Where is the ...?	... yùu sǎi	... ຢູ່ໃສ
How far is the ...?	... kai thao dai	... ໄກເທົ່າໃດ
I'm looking for the ...	khàwy sâwk hǎa ...	ຂ້ອຍຊອກຫາ ...
art gallery	háan wáang sá-daeng sǐ-la-pá	ຮ້ານວາງສະແດງ ສິລະປະ
barber shop	háan tát phǒm	ຮ້ານຕັດຜົມ
Buddhist temple; monastery	wat	ວັດ
cemetery	paa sâa	ປ່າຊ້າ
church	bòht khlit	ໂບດຄລິດ
city centre	kaang méuang	ກາງເມືອງ
... consulate	... kong-sǔun	... ກົງສຸນ
... embassy	... sa-thǎan-thûut	... ສະຖານທູດ
factory	hóhng ngáan	ໂຮງງານ
hotel	hóhng háem	ໂຮງແຮມ
market	ta-làat	ຕະຫລາດ
monument	á-nu-sǎa-wa-líi	ອານຸສາວະລີ
museum	phi-phit-tha-phán	ພິພິດທະພັນ
park (garden)	sǔan sǎa-tháa-la-na	ສວນສາທາລະນະ
police	tam-lùat	ຕຳຫລວດ
post office	pai-sá-níi (hóhng sǎai)	ໄປສະນີ (ໂຮງສາຍ)
public telephone	thóh-la-sáp sǎa-tháa-la-na	ໂທລະສັບ ສາທາລະນະ
public toilet	hàwng nâm sǎa-tháa-la-na	ຫ້ອງນ້ຳ ສາທາລະນະ
school	hóhng hían	ໂຮງຮຽນ
telephone centre	sǔun thóh-la-sáp	ສູນໂທລະສັບ
tourist information office	hàwng khàw múun khao sǎan thawng thiaw	ຫ້ອງຂໍ ມູນຂາວສານ ທ່ອງທ່ຽວ

AT THE BANK   ຢູ່ທະນາຄານ

The official national currency in the LPDR is the kip (ກີບ, kìip).
In reality, the people of Laos use three currencies in day-to-day
commerce: kip, Thai baht and US dollars. Kip notes come in
denominations of 100, 500, 1000, 2000 and 5000.

By and large, the best exchange rates are available at banks rather
than moneychangers. Travellers cheques receive a slightly better
exchange rate than cash. Banks in larger towns can change Euros,
Canadian, US and Australian dollars, French francs, Thai baht
and Japanese yen, while provincial banks will accept only US
dollars or baht.

Many hotels, upscale restaurants and gift shops in Vientiane
and Luang Prabang accept Visa or MasterCard. A few also accept
American Express.

I want to change money.
      khàwy yàak pian ngóen   ຂ້ອຍຢາກປ່ຽນເງິນ
Can I/we change money here?
      pian ngóen yuu níi dâi baw   ປ່ຽນເງິນຢູ່ນີ້ໄດ້ບໍ່
What is the exchange rate?
      át-taa lâek pian thao dại   ອັດຕາແລກປ່ຽນເທົ່າໃດ
Can I get smaller change?
      khǎw pian ngóen nâwy dâi baw   ຂໍປ່ຽນເງິນນ້ອຍໄດ້ບໍ່

I want to change ...   khàwy yàak pian ...   ຂ້ອຍຢາກປ່ຽນ ...
      cash/money   ngóen sót/ngóen   ເງິນສົດ/ເງິນ
      a cheque   bại saek   ໃບແຊັກ
      a travellers cheque saek thawng thiaw ແຊັກທ່ອງທ່ຽວ

Can I use my credit card to
withdraw money?
      khàwy sâi bát khléh-dít   ຂ້ອຍໃຊ້ບັດຄຣເດິດ
      thǎwn ngóen dâi baw   ຖອນເງິນໄດ້ບໍ່
What's your commission?
      jào ào khàa bàw-li-kàan   ເຈົ້າເອົາຄ່າບໍລິການເທົ່າໃດ
      thao dại

How many kip per dollar?
ják kìip taw dǒh-láa
ຈັກກີບ

Can I get smaller change?
khǎw pian ngóen nâwy
dâi baw
ຂໍປ່ຽນເງິນນ້ອຍໄດ້ບໍ່

Can I transfer money here from
my bank?
khàwy ǫhn ngóen jàak
tha-náa-kháan khàwy
máa nîi dâi baw
ຂ້ອຍໂອນເງິນຈາກ
ທະນາຄານຂ້ອຍ
ມານີ້ໄດ້ບໍ່

How many days will it take
to arrive?
ják méu sii máa hâwt
ຈັກມື້ຊິມາຣອດ

Has my money arrived yet?
ngóen khàwy máa
hâwt lâew baw
ເງິນຂ້ອຍມາຣອດແລ້ວບໍ່

Can I transfer money overseas?
khàwy ǫhn ngóen pai taang
pá-thêht dâi baw
ຂ້ອຍໂອນເງິນໄປຕ່າງໆ
ປະເທດໄດ້ບໍ່

I have ...	khàwy míi ...	ຂ້ອຍມີ ...
US$	dǫh-láa ạa-méh-li-kạa	ໂດລາອາເມລິກາ
UK£	pạwn ạng-kít	ປອນອັງກິດ
A$	dǫh-láa ạw-sá-tạa-líi	ໂດລາອິດສຕາລີ
HK$	dǫh-láa hong kọng	ໂດລາຮົງກົງ
Euros	yúu-lóh	ຢູໂລ
¥en	yéhn nyii-pun	ເຢັນຍີ່ປຸ່ນ

bank	tha-náa-kháan	ທະນາຄານ
change (n)	ngóen nâwy	ເງິນນ້ອຍ
to change	lâek pian	ແລກປ່ຽນ
check	saek	ແຊັກ
exchange rate	át-tạa lâek pian	ອັດຕາແລກປ່ຽນ
money	ngóen	ເງິນ

AT THE POST OFFICE   ຢູ່ທ້ອງການໄປສະນີ

Outgoing mail is fairly reliable and inexpensive. The safe arrival
of incoming mail is less certain, especially for packages. When
posting any package, even small padded mailers, you must leave
the package open for inspection by a postal officer.

Is this the post office?

nîi maen pai-sá-níi baw		ນີ້ແມ່ນໄປສະນີບໍ່

I want to send a ...	khàwy yàak song ...	ຂ້ອຍຢາກສົ່ງ ...
letter	jót-mǎai	ຈົດໝາຍ
postcard	pai-sá-níi bát	ໄປສະນີບັດ
parcel	haw kheuang	ຫໍເຄື່ອງ
telegram	thóh-la-lêhk	ໂທລະເລກ

Please send it by airmail/
surface mail.

ká-lu-náa song tháang	ກະລຸນາສົ່ງທາງ
aa-kàat/thám-ma-dáa	ອາກາດ/ທຳມະດາ

How much does it cost to
send this to ...?

láa-kháa thao-dai sǎm-láp	ລາຄາເທົ່າໃດສຳລັບ
song an-níi pai ...	ສົ່ງອັນນີ້ໄປ ...

May I have (a/an/some) ...?	khǎw ...	ຂໍ ...
stamps	sa-taem	ສະແຕມ
envelope	sáwng jót-mǎai	ຊອງຈົດໝາຍ
insurance	pá-kan phái	ປະກັນໄພ
registered receipt	bai lóng tha-bian	ໃບລົງທະບຽນ

This letter is going to the (USA).
   jót-mǎai nîi pại
   (ạa-méh-li-kạa)

จิดໝາຍນີ້ໄປ
ອາເມລິກາ

How much to send this letter
to (England)?
   song jót-mǎai nîi pại
   (ạng-kít) láa-kháa thao dại

ສົ່ງຈິດໝາຍນີ້ໄປອັງກິດ
ລາຄາເທົ່າໃດ

I'd like four 100 kip stamps, please.
   khǎw sa-taem bại-la
   hàwy kìip sii ạn

ຂໍສະແຕມໃບລະ
ຮ້ອຍກີບສີ່ອັນ

I want to send this package
by air mail.
   khàwy yàak song haw
   nîi pại tháang ạa-kàat

ຂ້ອຍຢາກສົ່ງຫໍ່ນີ້ໄປ
ທາງອາກາດ

I want a registered receipt.
   khàwy yàak dâi bại
   lóng tha-bịan

ຂ້ອຍຢາກໄດ້ໃບລົງ
ທະບຽນ

Where's the poste restante section?
   pawng bạw-li-kạan jót-mǎai
   sua kháo yuu sǎi

ປ່ອງບໍລິການຈິດໝາຍ
ຊົ່ວຄາວຢູ່ໃສ

Is there any mail for me?
   míi jót-mǎai khàwy baw

ມີຈິດໝາຍຂ້ອຍບໍ່

My last name is ...
   náam sá-kụn khàwy máen ...

ນາມສະກຸນຂ້ອຍແມ່ນ ...

AROUND TOWN

Useful Words

ຄຳສັບທີ່ເປັນປະໂຫຍດ

air (mail)	tháang ạa-kàat	ທາງອາກາດ
express (mail)	tháang duan	ທາງດ່ວນ
mail (n)	jót-mǎai	ຈິດໝາຍ
mail box	tûu jót-mǎai	ຕູ້ຈິດໝາຍ
postcode	la-hat pại-sa-níi	ລະຫັດໄປສະນີ
to register	lóng tha-bịan	ລົງທະບຽນ
registered mail	jót-mǎai long tha-bịan	ຈິດໝາຍລົງ ທະບຽນ
surface mail	jót-mǎai tháang	ຈິດໝາຍທາງ
	thám-ma-dạa	ທຳມະດາ

TELEPHONE   ໂທລະສັບ

The best place to make international calls is the International Telephone Office (Cabines Télécommuniques Internationales) on Thanon Setthathirat in Vientiane, which is open 24 hours a day. In provincial capitals, international telephone service is available at the GPO.

international call	thóh-la-sáp la-waang	ໂທລະສັບ
	pá-thêht	ລະຫວ່າງປະເທດ
long distance (domestic)	tháang kại	ທາງໄກ
minute(s)	náa-thíi	ມາທີ
mobile/cell phone	thóh-la-sáp méu thěu	ໂທລະສັບມືຖື
operator	phùu taw sǎi	ຜູ້ຕໍ່ສາຍ
phone book	pêum thóh-la-sáp	ປຶ້ມໂທລະສັບ
phone box	káp thóh-la-sáp	ກັບໂທລະສັບ
phonecard	bát thóh-la-sáp	ບັດໂທລະສັບ
telephone	thóh-la-sáp	ໂທລະສັບ
urgent	duan	ດ່ວນ

How much does it cost to
call Australia ...?

    thóh-la-sáp pại ạw-sá-tạa-líi   ໂທລະສັບໄປອົສຕາລິ
    láa-kháa thao dại   ລາຄາເທົ່າໃດ

I want to call ...

    khàwy yàak thóh ...   ຂ້ອຍຢາກໂທ ...

I'd like to speak for 10 minutes.

    khàwy yàak thóh síp náa-thíi   ຂ້ອຍຢາກໂທສິບມາທີ

How much does a (three)-minute
call cost?

    khaa thóh (sǎam) náa-thíi   ຄ່າໂທ(ສາມ)ມາທີ
    thao dại   ເທົ່າໃດ

How much does each extra
minute cost?
    kháa thóh phôem náa-thii   ຄ່າໂທເພີ່ມມາທີລະເທົ່າໃດ
    la thao dại
The number is ...
    bọe thóh maen ...   ເບີໂທແມ່ນ ...
It's engaged.
    thóh-la-sáp baw waang   ໂທລະສັບບໍ່ຫວ່າງໆ
I've been cut off.
    thóh-la-sáp tàt   ໂທລະສັບຕັດ

FAX & TELEGRAPH   ໂທລະສານແລະໂທລະເລກ

Fax, telex and telegraph services are handled at the GPO in each
provincial capital. Larger hotels with business centres offer the
same telecommunication services but always at higher rates.

How much per page?
    phaen-la thao dại   ແຜ່ນລະເທົ່າໃດ
How much per word?
    khám-la thao dại   ຄຳລະເທົ່າໃດ

fax	fáek	ແຟັກ
telegraph	thóh-la-lêhk	ໂທລະເລກ

INTERNET   ອິນເຕີແນັດ

Is there a local Internet cafe?
    míi ịn-tọe-naet kạa-féh baw   ມີອິນເຕີແນັດກາເຟບໍ່
I'd like to get Internet access.
    khàwy yàak sải ịn-tọe-naet   ຂ້ອຍຢາກໃຊ້ອິນເຕີແນັດ
I'd like to check my email.
    yàak kùat ịi-máew   ຢາກກວດອິແມວ
I'd like to send an email.
    yàak song ịi-máew   ຢາກສົ່ງອິແມວ

computer	kháwm-pịi-tọe	ຄອມປິຕີ
email	ịi-máew	ອິແມວ
modem	móh-dạem	ໂມແດມ

PAPERWORK ເອກະສານ

name	seu	ຊື່
address	thii yuu	ທີ່ຢູ່
date of birth	wán dẹuan pịi kòet	ວັນເດືອນປີເກິດ
place of birth	thii kòet	ທີ່ເກິດ
age	ạa-nyu	ອາຍຸ
sex	phêht	ເພດ
nationality	sǎn-sâat	ສັນຊາດ
religion	sàat-sá-náa	ສາສະນາ
profession/work	ạa-sîip	ອາຊີບ
reason for travel	jút-pa-sǒng dẹon tháang	ຈຸດປະສົງເດີນທາງ
customs	dàan pháa-sǐi	ດ່ານພາສີ
marital status	thǎa-na kạan	ຖານະ
	taeng-ngáan	ການແຕ່ງງານ
single	sòht	ໂສດ
married	taeng-ngáan lâew	ແຕ່ງງານແລ້ວ
divorced	hâang lâew	ຮ້າງແລ້ວ
widow	mae màai	ແມ່ໝ້າຍ
widower	phaw màai	ພໍ່ໝ້າຍ
identification	bát pá-jạm tụa	ບັດປະຈຳຕົວ
passport number	nâm-bọe nǎng sěu	ນ້ຳເບີ
	phaan dẹen	ໜັງສືຜ່ານແດນ
visa	wi-sáa	ວິຊາ
drivers licence	bại á-nu-nyâat kháp khii	ໃບອະນຸຍາດຂັບຂີ່
immigration	kùat khón khào méuang	ກວດຄົນເຂົ້າເມືອງ
purpose of visit	jút pa-sǒng yîam yáam	ຈຸດປະສົງຢ້ຽມຍາມ
business	thu-la-kít	ທຸລະກິດ
holiday	phak phawn	ພັກຜ່ອນ
visiting relatives	yáam phii-nâwng	ຍາມພີ່ນ້ອງ
visiting the homeland	yáam bâan kòet	ຍາມບ້ານເກິດ

SIGHTSEEING

ການທ່ອງຊົມ

Where's the tourist office?
    hàwng kaan thawng thiaw
    yuu sǎi

ຫ້ອງການທ່ອງທ່ຽວຢູ່ໃສ

Do you have a local map?
    míi phǎen-thii tua méuang baw

ມີແຜນທີ່ຕົວເມືອງບໍ່

Do you have a guidebook in English?
    míi pêum nám thiaw pháa sǎa
    ang-kít baw

ມີປື້ມນຳທ່ຽວພາສາ
ອັງກິດບໍ່

What are the main attractions?
    laeng thawng thiaw thii
    sǎm-khán maen nyǎng

ແຫລ່ງທ່ອງທ່ຽວທີ່ສຳຄັນ
ແມ່ນຫຍັງ

Can we take photographs?
    thaai hûup dâi baw

ຖ່າຍຮູບໄດ້ບໍ່

I'll send you the photograph.
    khàwy síi fàak hûup máa hâi

ຂ້ອຍຊິຝາກຮູບມາໃຫ້

What time does it open/close?
    poet/pít wéh-láa ják móhng

ເປີດ/ປິດເວລາຈັກໂມງ

Is there an admission charge?
    kép khaa phaan pa-tuu baw

ເກັບຄ່າຜ່ານປະຕູບໍ່

Is there a discount for ...?	lut láa-kháa săm-láp ... baw	ລຸດລາຄາ ສຳລັບ ... ບໍ່
children	dék nâwy	ເດັກນ້ອຍ
students	nak hían	ນັກຮຽນ

What's that building?
nân maen ąa-kháan nyăng   ນັ້ນແມ່ນອາຄານຫຍັງ
What's this monument?
nii maen   ນີ້ແມ່ນ
ąa-nu-săa-wa-líi nyăng   ອານຸສາວະລິຫຍັງ
What's that?
nân maen nyăng   ນັ້ນແມ່ນຫຍັງ
How old is it?
ąa-nyu ják pịi lâew   ອາຍຸຈັກປີແລ້ວ

WHAT'S A WAT?

Technically speaking, the wat (ວັດ) is a compound where Buddhist monks and/or nuns reside. In Laos, a typical wat may contain the following structures:

drum tower	hăw kąwng	ຫໍກອງ
ordination hall	sĭm	ສິມ
monastic quarters	kú-tí	ກຸຕິ
stupa	thâat	ທາດ

'bone stupas', where the ashes of worshippers are interred
thâat ká-dùuk   ທາດກະດູກ

pavilion, where laity listen to thám or Buddhist doctrine
săa-láa fáng thám   ສາລາຟັງທຳ

spirit house, for the temple's reigning earth spirit
hăw phĭi khún wat   ຫໍຜີຄຸນວັດ

Tipitaka library, where Buddhist scriptures are stored
hăw tại   ຫໍໄຕ

Buddhist temple	wat	ວັດ
cave	thám	ຖ້ຳ
memorial	ąa-nu-sǎwn	ອານຸສອນສະຖານ
	sa-thǎan	
museum	phi-phit-tha-phán	ພິພິດທະພັນ
national	khèt á-nu-lak	ເຂດອະນຸລັກ
biodiversity	síi-wa-náa-phán	ຊີວະນາພັນ
conservation	haeng sâat	ແຫ່ງຊາດ
area (NBCA)		
national park	sǔan ut-thi-yáan	ສວນອຸທິຍານ
	haeng sâat	ແຫ່ງຊາດ
palace	pha-láa-sa-wáng	ພະລາຊະວັງ
shrine	hǎw wâi	ຫໍໄຫວ້
spirit house	hǎw phǐi	ຫໍຜີ
statue	hûup pán	ຮູບປັ້ນ
stupa	thâat	ທາດ
university	ma-hǎa-wi-tha-nyáa-lái	ມະຫາວິທະຍາໄລ
waterfall	nâm tók tàat	ນ້ຳຕົກຕາດ
zoo	sǔan sát	ສວນສັດ

AROUND TOWN

SIGNS

ຮ້ອນ	HOT
ເຢັນ	COLD
ທາງເຂົ້າ	ENTRANCE
ທາງອອກ	EXIT
ເປີດ	OPEN
ອັດ/ປິດ	CLOSED
ຫ້າມເຂົ້າ	NO ENTRY
ຫ້າມສູບຢາ	NO SMOKING
ຫ້າມ	PROHIBITED
ຫ້ອງນ້ຳ	TOILETS

WAT'S THE STORY?

Correct behaviour in a wat entails several guidelines, the most important of which is to dress neatly (no shorts or sleeveless shirts) and to take your shoes off when you enter any building that contains a Buddha image. Buddha images are sacred objects, so don't pose in front of them for pictures and definitely do not clamber upon them.

Monks are not supposed to touch or be touched by women. If a woman wants to hand something to a monk, the object should be placed within reach of the monk, not handed directly to him.

When sitting in a religious edifice, keep your feet pointed away from any Buddha images or monks. The usual way to do this is to sit in the 'mermaid' pose in which your legs are folded to the side, with the feet pointing backwards.

AROUND TOWN

BARGAINING   ການຕໍ່ລອງລາຄາ

Negotiating prices, ie, bargaining, is a common practice in Laos, as in most of South-East Asia. You can expect to bargain for most items offered for sale in a market, even when prices are posted. In department stores and convenience shops, however, prices are fixed. Don't go overboard when bargaining – both seller and buyer lose face when you argue too vehemently or haggle over a few kìip (ກີບ).

How much?	thao dại	ເທົ່າໃດ
How many kip?	ják kìip	ຈັກກີບ

Do you have something cheaper?
    míi aạn thèuk-kwaa nîi baw   ມີອັນຖືກກວ່ານີ້ບໍ່

The price is very high.
    láa-kháa pháeng lǎai   ລາຄາແພງຫລາຍ

I think that's too much.
    khit waa pháeng phôht   ຄິດວ່າແພງໂພດ

Can you bring the price down?
    lut láa-kháa dâi baw   ລຸດລາຄາໄດ້ບໍ່

Can you lower it more?
    lut ìik dâi baw   ລຸດອີກໄດ້ບໍ່

How about ... kip?
    ... kìip dâi baw   ... ກີບໄດ້ບໍ່

I don't have much money.
    khàwy baw míi ngóen lǎai   ຂ້ອຍບໍ່ມີເງິນຫລາຍ

If I/we buy two ... (+ classifier)
will you lower the price?
    thàa sêu sǎwng ... lut dâi baw   ຖ້າຊື້ສອງ ... ລຸດໄດ້ບໍ່

The quality is not very good.
    khún-na-phâap baw dịi pạan dại   ຄຸນນະພາບບໍ່ດີປານໃດ

What's your lowest price?
    láa-kháa tam sút thao dại   ລາຄາຕໍ່າສຸດເທົ່າໃດ

MAKING A PURCHASE   ການຈັດຊຶ

Do you have any ...?	mįi ... baw	ມີ ... ບໍ່
Please give me ...	khăw ...	ຂໍ ...
I'm looking for ...	khàwy sàwk hăa ...	ຂອຍຊອກຫາ ...
Do you have any more?	mįi ìik baw	ມີອິກບໍ່
I'd like to see another style.	khăw boeng ìik bàep neung	ຂໍເບິ່ງອິກແບບໜຶ່ງ

How much (for) ...?	... thao dại	... ເທົ່າໃດ
both	tháng săwng	ທັງສອງ
per fruit	nuay-la	ໜວຍລະ
per metre	maet-la	ແມັດລະ
per piece	ạn-la	ອັນລະ
this	ạn-nîi	ອັນນີ້
three pieces	săam ạn	ສາມອັນ

How much altogether?
    thuk yaang thao dại   ທຸກຢ່າງໆເທົ່າໃດ

I'd like (a) ...	khàwy tâwng-kạan ...	ຂ້ອຍຕ້ອງການ ...
Where can	já hăa ...	ຈະຫາ ...
I find (a) ...?	dâi yuu săi	ໄດ້ຢູ່ໃສ
batteries	thaan fái săi	ຖ່ານໄຟສາຍ
bread	khào jii	ເຂົ້າຈີ່
butter	bǫe	ເບີ
candles	thían	ທຽນ
cheese	nóei khǎeng	ເນີຍແຂງ
chocolate	sawk-kǫh-laet	ຊ້ອກໂກແລັດ
eggs	khai	ໄຂ່
flour	pâeng	ແປ້ງ
gas cyclinder	thǎng káet	ຖັງແກ໊ສ
ham	háem	ແຮມ
honey	nâm phòeng	ນ້ຳເຜິ້ງ
margarine	mâak-kạa-lín	ມາກກາລິນ

matches	káp-khìit	ກັບຂີດ
milk	nâm nóm	ນ້ຳນົມ
mosquito coil	yạa jùt nyúng	ຢາຈຸດຍຸງ
mosquito repellant	yạa kạn nyúng	ຢາກັນຍຸງ
pepper	màak phét	ໝາກເຜັດ
salt	kẹua	ເກືອ
shampoo	yạa sa hǔa	ຢາຊະຫົວ
soap	sá-bùu	ສະບູ
sugar	nâm tạan	ນ້ຳຕານ
toilet paper	jìa hàwng nâm	ເຈ້ຍຫ້ອງນ້ຳ
toothpaste	yạa thúu khàew	ຢາຖູແຂ້ວ
washing powder	fâep	ແຟບ

SOUVENIRS & CRAFTS

ເຄື່ອງທິລະລຶກແລະເຄື່ອງ
ຂັດຖະກຳ

Hill-tribe crafts abound in Laos, and make fine souvenirs of your travels. Like elsewhere in South-East Asia, bargaining is a local tradition (originally introduced to the area by early Arab and Indian traders). Although most shops nowadays have fixed prices, fabric, carvings, jewellery and antiques are usually subject to bargaining.

The Lao produce well-crafted carvings in wood, bone and stone. Subjects can be anything from Hindu or Buddhist mythology to themes from everyday life. Opium pipes seem to be plentiful in Laos and sometimes have intricately carved bone or bamboo shafts, along with engraved ceramic bowls. Vientiane, Luang Prabang, Pakse and Savannakhet each have a sprinkling of antique shops. Anything that looks old could be up for sale in these shops, including Asian pottery (especially Ming dynasty porcelain), old jewellery, clothes, carved wood, musical instruments, coins and bronze statuettes.

baskets	ká-taa	ກະຕ່າ
handicrafts	kheuang hát-thá-kạm	ເຄື່ອງຫັດຖະກຳ
pottery/ceramics	kheuang dìn	ເຄື່ອງດິນ

MATERIALS

ວັດຖຸ

What is this made of?

nîi het dûay nyǎng   ນີ້ເຮັດດ້ວຍຫຍັງ

aluminium	áa-lúu-míi-níam	ອາລູມິນຽມ
brass	tháwng lěuang	ທອງເຫລືອງ
bronze	tháwng sǎm-lít	ທອງສຳລິດ
cloth	phàa	ຜ້າ
copper	tháwng dạeng	ທອງແດງ
gold (pure)	khám	ຄຳ

gold-plated	khám bại	ຄຳໃບ
leather	năng	ໜັງ
silver	ngóen	ເງິນ
stone	hĭn	ຫີນ
teak	mâi sák	ໄມ້ສັກ
wood	mâi	ໄມ້

LAO LOOMS

All together Laos is said to have some 16 basic weaving styles divided among four basic regions. Southern weavers, who often use foot looms rather than frame looms, practise Laos' most continuous textile traditions in terms of styles and patterns, some of which haven't changed for a century or more. Southern Laos is known for the best silk weaving and for intricate mat-mĭi (ikat or tie-dye) designs that include Khmer-influenced temple and elephant motifs. Synthetic and natural dyes are commonly used.

In north-eastern Laos (especially Hua Phan's Sam Neua and Xieng Khuang's Muang Phuan) the Thai Neua, Phuan, Thai Lü, Thai Daeng, Thai Dam and Phu Thai mainly produce weft brocade (yìap kò) using raw silk, cotton yarn and natural dyes, sometimes with the addition of mat-mĭi techniques. Large diamond patterns are common.

In central Laos, typical weavings include indigo-dyed cotton mat-mĭi and minimal weft brocade (jók and khít), along with techniques borrowed from all over the country (brought by migrants to Vientiane – many of whom fled war zones). Gold and silver brocade is typical of traditional Luang Prabang patterns, along with intricate patterns (lái) and imported Thai Lü designs.

Northerners generally use frame looms; the waist, body and bottom border of a phàa nung or sarong are often sewn together from separately woven pieces.

TEXTILES ຜ້າແພ

Silk and cotton fabrics are woven in many different styles according to the geographic provenance and ethnicity of the weavers.

cotton	phàa fàai	ຜ້າຝ້າຍ
embroidery	phàa thák saew	ຜ້າທັກແຊ່ວ
ikat-style tie-dyed cloth	mat-mii	ມັດໝີ່
minimal weft brocade	jók/khít	ຈົກ/ຂິດ
silk	phàa mǎi	ຜ້າໄໝ
shoulder bag	thǒng pháai	ຖົງພາຍ
traditional long sarong for women	sìin	ສິ້ນ

GEMS & JEWELLERY ເພັດພອຍ ແລະ ເຄື່ອງປະດັບ

Gold and silver jewellery is a good buy in Laos, although you must search hard for well-made pieces. Some of the best silverwork is done by the hill tribes. Gems are also sometimes available, but you can get better prices in Thailand.

Most provincial towns have a few shops that specialise in jewellery. You can also find jewellery in antique and handicraft shops.

bracelet	sǎi khǎen	ສາຍແຂນ
diamond	phet	ເພັດ
emerald	kâew máw-la-kót	ແກ້ວມໍລະກົດ
gems	phet pháwy	ເພັດພອຍ
jade	nyók	ຫຍົກ
necklace	sǎai kháw	ສາຍຄໍ
ring	wǎen	ແຫວນ
ruby	thap thím	ທັບທິມ
sapphire	pháwy sǐi kháam	ພອຍສີຄາມ
silver	ngóen	ເງິນ

CLOTHING ເຄື່ອງ

The general Lao word for clothing is sèua phàa (ເສື້ອຜ້າ). Sèua (ເສື້ອ) itself can mean 'shirt', 'blouse', 'dress' or 'jacket'; phàa (ຜ້າ) means 'cloth'.

hat	mùak	ໝວກ
shirt/blouse/ jacket/dress	sèua	ເສື້ອ
shoes	kòep	ເກີບ
skirt (Lao-style)	sìin	ສິ້ນ
skirt (Western-style)	ká-pohng	ກະໂປ່ງ
socks	thŏng thǎo	ຖົງເທົ້າ
style	bàep	ແບບ
tailor	saang tát kheuang	ຊ່າງຕັດເຄື່ອງ
trousers	sòng khǎa nyáo	ສົ້ງຂາຍາວ
underwear	sòng sâwn	ສົ້ງຊ້ອນ

Can you make ...?	tát ... dâi baw	ຕັດ ... ໄດ້ບໍ່
The sleeves are too ...	khǎen ... phôht	ແຂນ ... ໂພດ
long	nyáo	ຍາວ
short	sàn	ສັ້ນ

FABRICS ຜ້າ

Synthetic materials and Western fabric weaves use the same names as in English (eg, polyester, dacron, serge, gabardine, etc), spoken with a Lao accent.

cotton	phàa fàai	ຜ້າຝ້າຍ
leather	nǎng	ໜັງ
linen	phàa lìi-nín	ຜ້າລິນິນ
silk	phàa mǎi	ຜ້າໄໝ
wool	phàa khǒn sát	ຜ້າຂົນສັດ

COLOURS

ສີ

dark	sǐi kae	ສີແກ່
light	sǐi awn	ສີອ່ອນ
black	sǐi dạm	ສີດຳ
blue	sǐi fâa	ສີຟ້າ
brown	sǐi nâm-tạan	ສີນ້ຳຕານ
green	sǐi khǐaw	ສີຂຽວ
grey	sǐi khìi thao	ສີຂີ້ເທົ່າ
pink	sǐi bụa	ສີບົວ
purple	sǐi muang	ສີມ່ວງ
red	sǐi dạeng	ສີແດງ
white	sǐi khǎo	ສີຂາວ
yellow	sǐi lěuang	ສີເຫລືອງ

Do you have another colour?
    míi sǐi eun baw   ມີສີອື່ນບໍ່

TOILETRIES

ເຄື່ອງສຳອາງ

brush	pạeng	ແປງ
comb	wǐi	ຫວີ
condoms	thǒng yạang á-náa-mái	ຖົງຢາງອະນາໄມ
dental floss	sêuak jǐim khàew	ເຊືອກຈິ້ມແຂ້ວ
deodorant	yạa kạn kin tụa	ຢາກັນກິ່ນຕົວ
moisturiser	khíim tháa nàa	ຄີມທາໜ້າ
razor	mìit thǎe	ມີດແຖ
razor blades	bại mìit thǎe	ໃບມີດແຖ
sanitary napkins	phàa á-náa-mái	ຜ້າອະນາໄມ
shampoo	nâm yạa sá phǒm	ນ້ຳຢາຊະຜົມ
shaving cream	yáa thǎe nùat	ຢາແຖໜວດ
soap	sá-bụu	ສະບູ
sunblock	yáa kạn dàet	ຢາກັນແດດ
tissues	jǐa á-náa-mái	ເຈ້ຍອະນາໄມ
toilet paper	jǐa hàwng nâm	ເຈ້ຍຫ້ອງນ້ຳ
toothbrush	pạeng thǔu khàew	ແປງຖູແຂ້ວ
toothpaste	yạa thǔu khàew	ຢາຖູແຂ້ວ

STATIONERY & PUBLICATIONS

ເຈ້ຍແລະສິ່ງພິມ

book	pêum	ປຶ້ມ
bookshop	hàan khǎai pêum	ຮ້ານຂາຍປຶ້ມ
envelope	sáwng jót-mǎai	ຊອງຈົດໝາຍ
guidebook	pêum thawng thiaw	ປຶ້ມທ່ອງທ່ຽວ
ink	nâm móek	ນ້ຳໝຶກ
magazine	wáa-la-sǎan	ວາລະສານ
newspaper	nǎng-sěu phím	ໜັງສືພິມ
notebook	pêum bạn théuk	ປຶ້ມບັນທຶກ
pen	bík	ບິກ
pencil	sǎw dạm	ສໍດຳ
stationery	keuang khǐan	ເຄື່ອງຂຽນ
writing paper	jîa khǐan	ເຈ້ຍຂຽນ

PHOTOGRAPHY

ການຖ່າຍຮູບ

camera	kâwng thaai húup	ກ້ອງຖ່າຍຮູບ
develop (photos)	lâang húup	ລ້າງຮູບ
lens	léhn	ເລນ
photograph	húup	ຮູບ
to photograph	thaai húup	ຖ່າຍຮູບ
film	fím húup	ຟິມຮູບ
colour	fím sǐi	ຟິມສີ
B&W	fím khǎo dạm	ຟິມຂາວດຳ
slide film	fím sá-lái	ຟິມສະໄລ

When will it be ready?
  wéh-láa-dại já lâang
  húup jóp lâew

ເວລາໃດຈະລ້າງ
ຮູບຈົບແລ້ວ

How many days?
  ják mêu

ຈັກມື້

SMOKING

ສູບຍາ

A packet of ... cigarettes, please.
  ao yạa sùup hài dae
  sáwng nèung

ເອົາຍາສູບໃຫ້ແດ່
ຊອງໜຶ່ງ

Are these cigarettes strong
or mild?
  yạa nîi púk lěu jạang

ຍານີ້ປຸກຫລືຈາງ

Do you have a light?
  míi káp fái baw

ມີກັບໄຟບໍ່

Please don't smoke.
  ká-lu-náa yạa sùup yáa

ກະລຸນາຍາສູບຍາ

Can I smoke?
  sùup yạa dâi baw

ສູບຍາໄດ້ບໍ່

cigarettes	yạa sùup	ຍາສູບ
cigarette papers	jìa phán yạa sùup	ເຈັ້ຍພັນຍາສູບ
filtered	kạwng	ກອງ
lighter	káp fái	ກັບໄຟ
matches	káp khìit	ກັບຂິດ
menthol	yáa sùup yén	ຍາສູບເຍັນ
pipe	kàwk	ກອກ
tobacco	yáa sèn	ຍາເສັ້ນ

ONE LOH OF BREAD

Don't forget to use a classifier when indicating a
number of something – the general-purpose classifier
that should get you through is loh. Find more
classifiers on page 43.

SHOPPING

WEIGHTS & MEASURES

ການຊັ່ງແລະການວັດແທກ

Dimensions and weight are usually expressed using the metric system in Laos. The exception is land measure, which is usually quoted using the traditional system of wáa, ngáan and hâi. Gold jewellery is often measured in baht (bàat).

1 wáa	= 4 sq metres	ວາ
1 ngáan (100 sq wáa)	= 400 sq metres	ງານ
1 hâi (4 ngáan)	= 1600 sq metres	ໄຮ່
1 bàat	= 15 grams	ບາດ

kilogram	kí-lóh	ກິໂລ
kilometre	kí-lóh-maet	ກິໂລແມັດ
metre	maet	ແມັດ
litre	liit	ລິດ

SIZES & COMPARISONS

ຂະໜາດແລະການສົມທຽບ

Do you have anything ... than this?	míi ... nîi baw	ມີ ... ນີ້ບໍ່
larger	nyai-kwaa	ໃหຍ່ກ່ວາ
smaller	nâwy-kwaa	ນ້ອຍກ່ວາ
too tight	kháp phôht	ຄັບໂພດ
too small	nâwy phôht	ນ້ອຍໂພດ
too large	nyai phôht	ໃຫຍ່ໂພດ
too wide	kwâang phôht	ກ້ວາງໂພດ
too long	nyáo phôht	ຍາວໂພດ
too short	sàn phôht	ສັ້ນໂພດ

SHOPPING

to bargain	taw	ຕໍ່
to buy	sêu	ຊື້
cheap	thèuk	ຖືກ
expensive	pháeng	ແພງ
quality	khún-na-phâap	ຄຸນນະພາບ
sell	khǎai	ຂາຍ
size	kha-nàat	ຂະຫນາດ

not enough	baw pháw	ບໍ່ພໍ
still not enough	nyáng baw pháw	ຍັງບໍ່ພໍ
good enough	pháw dịi	ພໍດີ

I'd like to see ...	yàak boeng ...	ຢາກເບິ່ງ ...
this one	ạn níi	ອັນນີ້
that one	ạn nân	ອັນນັ້ນ

Which one?		
ạn dại		ອັນໃດ
Do you have any more?		
míi iik baw		ມີອີກບໍ່

Lao cuisine is similar to Thai cuisine in many ways. Almost all dishes are cooked using fresh ingredients, including vegetables, fish, poultry, pork and beef or water buffalo.

Except for one-dish rice plates and noodle dishes, Lao meals are usually ordered family style, which is to say that two or more people order together, sharing different dishes. Traditionally, the party orders one of each kind of dish, eg, one salad, one stir-fry, one soup, etc. Each dish is generally large enough for two people. Extras may be ordered for a large party.

Because of Laos' distance from the sea, freshwater fish is more commonly used than saltwater fish or shellfish. To salt the food, various fermented fish concoctions are used, most commonly nâm pąa (ນ້ຳປາ), which is a thin sauce of fermented anchovies (usually imported from Thailand), and pąa dàek (ປາແດກ), a coarser, native Lao preparation that includes chunks of fermented freshwater fish, rice husks and rice 'dust'. Nâm pąa dàek (ນ້ຳປາແດກ) is the sauce poured from pąa dàek.

Many Lao dishes are quite spicy because of the Lao penchant for chillies or màak phét (ໝາກເຜັດ). But the Lao also eat a lot of what could be called Chinese food which is generally, but not always, less spicy.

Rice is the foundation for all Lao meals (as opposed to snacks), as elsewhere in South-East Asia. In general, the Lao eat 'sticky' or glutinous rice (ເຂົ້າໜຽວ, khào nǐaw), although ordinary steamed white rice (ເຂົ້າໜຶ່ງ, khào nèung) is also common. Sticky rice is served in lidded baskets and eaten with the hands: the general practice is to grab a small fistful from the woven container that sits on the table, then roll it into a rough ball which is used to dip into the various dishes. Khào nèung, on the other hand, is eaten with a fork and spoon. The fork is only used to prod food onto the spoon, which is the main utensil for eating this type of rice. Chopsticks (ໄມ້ທູ່, mâi thuu) are only used for eating fǒe (ເຝີ) or other Chinese noodle dishes.

FOOD

AT THE RESTAURANT
ຢູ່ຮ້ານອາຫານ

Please bring (a) ...	khǎw ... dae	ຂໍ ... ແດ່
bill	saek	ແຊັກ
bowl	thùay	ຖ້ວຍ
chopsticks	mâi thuu	ໄມ້ທູ່
fork	sâwm	ສ້ອມ
glass	jàwk	ຈອກ
knife	mîit	ມີດ
menu	láai-kan ạa-hǎan	ລາຍການອາຫານ
plate	jaan	ຈານ
spoon	buang	ບ່ວງ

I don't like it hot and spicy.
  baw mak phét — ບໍ່ມັກເຜັດ
I like it hot and spicy.
  mak phét — ມັກເຜັດ
I can eat Lao food.
  kịn ạa-hǎan láo dâi — ກິນອາຫານລາວໄດ້
Do you have ...?
  míi ... baw — ມີ ... ບໍ່
What do you have that's special?
  míi nyǎng phi-sèt baw — ມີຫຍັງພິເສດບໍ່
I'd like to try that.
  khàwy yàak láwng kịn boeng — ຂ້ອຍຢາກລອງກິນເບິ່ງ
I didn't order this.
  khàwy baw dâi sang náew níi — ຂ້ອຍບໍ່ໄດ້ສັ່ງແນວນີ້

| delicious | sâep | ແຊບ |

WIT & WISDOM

It's easy to earn money but difficult to find kindness.

ngóen khám hǎa dâi,	ເງິນຄຳຫາໄດ້
nâm jai hǎa yàak	ນ້ຳໃຈຫາຍາກ

VEGETARIAN MEALS ອາຫານເຈ

Those visitors who wish to avoid eating animal food while in Laos can be accommodated only with extreme effort. Chinese restaurants are your best bet since many Chinese Buddhists eat vegetarian food during Buddhist festivals. More often than not, however, visiting vegetarians are left to their own devices at the average restaurant. In Lao the magic words are:

FOOD

I eat only vegetables.
  khàwy kịn tae phák ຂ້ອຍກິນແຕ່ຜັກ
I can't eat pork.
  khàwy kịn mǔu baw dâi ຂ້ອຍກິນຊີ້ນໝູບໍ່ໄດ້
I can't eat beef.
  khàwy kịn sìin ngúa baw dâi ຂ້ອຍກິນງົວບໍ່ໄດ້
I don't want any meat.
  khàwy baw ạo sìin sát ຂ້ອຍບໍ່ເອົາຊີ້ນສັດ
No fish or chicken.
  baw sai pạa lěu kai ບໍ່ໃສ່ປາຫລືໄກ່
I/We want vegetables only.
(see Vegetables, page 111)
  ạo phák thao nân ເອົາຜັກເທົ່ານັ້ນ
Please don't use fish sauce.
  ká-lu-náa baw sai nâm pạa ກະລຸນາບໍ່ໃສ່ນ້ຳປາ
Please don't use padaek.
  ká-lu-náa baw sai pạa dàek ກະລຸນາບໍ່ໃສ່ປາແດກ
Please don't use MSG.
  ká-lu-náa baw sai pâeng núa ກະລຸນາບໍ່ໃສ່ແປ້ງນົວ

soy sauce nâm sá-îu ນ້ຳສະອິ້ວ
tofu (soybean curd) tào-hûu ເຕົ້າຮູ້
vegetable oil nâm-mán phêut ນ້ຳມັນພືດ

FOOD

STAPLES ການລາເຝ

beef	sìn ngúa	ຊີ້ນງົວ
chicken	kai	ໄກ່
fish	paa	ປາ
pork	sìn mǔu	ຊີ້ນໝູ
rice	khào	ເຂົ້າ
seafood	aa-hǎan tha-léh	ອາຫານທະເລ
shrimp/prawns	kûng	ກຸ້ງ
vegetables	phak	ຜັກ
water buffalo	sìn khuáai	ຊີ້ນຄວາຍ

RICE DISHES ອາຫານກັບເຂົ້າ

steamed white rice	khào nèung	ເຂົ້າໜຶ້ງ
sticky rice	khào nǐaw	ເຂົ້າໜຽວ
curry over rice	khào làat kaeng	ເຂົ້າລາດແກງ
'red' pork (char siu) with rice	khào mǔu daeng	ເຂົ້າໝູແດງ
roast duck over rice	khào nàa pét	ເຂົ້າໜ້າເປັດ
fried rice with ...	khào phát (khào khùa) ...	ເຂົ້າຜັດ (ເຂົ້າຂົ້ວ) ...
chicken	kai	ໄກ່
pork	mǔu	ໝູ
shrimp/prawns	kûng	ກຸ້ງ
crab	puu	ປູ

NOODLES   ເຝີ/ໝີ່

Fŏe (ເຝີ), perhaps the most common food sold anywhere in Laos, are flat noodles made with rice flour. Heavier wheat noodles – sometimes made with egg, sometimes not – are known as mii (ໝີ່). You'll find both kinds noodles in most Lao restaurants and in small hàan fŏe (noodle shops). Slivers of beef or pork are the usual accompaniments, though occasionally chicken may be available. Because of their Chinese origins, noodles are usually eaten with chopsticks (and a spoon if served in a broth).

Fŏe is quite popular as a snack or even for breakfast, and is almost always served with a plate of fresh lettuce, mint, coriander, mung-bean sprouts, lime wedges and sometimes basil, for adding to the soup as desired. In some places – especially in the south – people mix their own fŏe sauce of lime, crushed fresh chilli, fermented shrimp paste (ກະປິ, ká-pí) and sugar at the table using a little saucer provided for that purpose.

fŏe	ເຝີ
rice noodle soup with vegetables and meat	
fŏe hàeng	ເຝີແຫ້ງ
rice noodles with vegetables and meat, no broth	
làat nàa	ລາດໜ້າ
rice noodles with gravy	
fŏe khùa	ເຝີຂົ້ວ
fried rice noodles with meat and vegetables	
phát sá-îu	ຜັດສະອິ້ວ
fried rice noodles with soy sauce	
mii nâm	ໝີ່ນ້ຳ
yellow wheat noodles in broth, with vegetables and meat	
mii hàeng	ໝີ່ແຫ້ງ
yellow wheat noodles with vegetables and meat	
khào pûn	ເຂົ້າປຸ້ນ
white flour noodles served with sweet-spicy sauce	

FOOD

BREAD & PASTRIES   ເຂົ້າຈີ່ ແລະ ເຂົ້າໜົມ

plain bread (usually French-style)
   khào jìi   ເຂົ້າຈີ່
baguette sandwich
   khào jìi páa-tê   ເຂົ້າຈີ່ປາເຕ
croissants
   khúa-sawng   ຄົວຊ່ອງ
'Chinese doughnuts'
   (Mandarin youtiao)
   pá-thawng-kó   ປະຖ່ອງໂກະ (ເຂົ້າໜົມຄູ່)
   (khào-nǒm khuu)

EGGS   ໄຂ່

egg	khai	ໄຂ່
fried egg	khai dạo	ໄຂ່ດາວ
hard-boiled egg	khai tôm	ໄຂ່ຕົ້ມ
plain omelette	jẹun khai	ຈືນໄຂ່
scrambled egg	khai khùa	ໄຂ່ຂົ້ວ

APPETISERS   ກັບແກ້ມ
('DRINKING FOOD')

Káp kêam (ກັບແກ້ມ) are dishes intended to be eaten on picnics or while drinking beer, lào láo (ເຫົ້າລາວ, rice alcohol) or other alcoholic beverages. English-language menus in Laos may translate such dishes as 'snacks' or 'appetisers'. You can also order káp kêam with regular meals, although they will usually be served before other kinds of dishes.

cellophane noodle salad	yám sèn wûn	ຍຳເສັ້ນທວຸນ
dried water buffalo skin	nǎng khuáai hàeng	ໜັງຄວາຍແຫ້ງ
fried peanuts	thua dịn jẹun	ຖົ່ວດິນຈືນ
fried potatoes	mán fa-lang jẹun	ມັນຝລັ່ງຈືນ

fresh spring rolls	yáw díp	ຍໍດິບ
fried spring rolls	yáw jęun	ຍໍຈືນ
shrimp chips	khào khìap kûng	ເຂົ້າຂຸບກຸ້ງ
spicy green papaya salad	tạm màak-hung	ຕຳໝາກຫຸ່ງ
spicy grilled chicken	pîng kai	ປີ້ງໄກ່
toasted pork	pîng mǔu	ປີ້ງໝູ

FOOD

MEAT SALADS   ລາບ

One of the most common Lao dishes is làap (ລາບ), which is a
salad of minced meat, chicken or fish tossed with lime juice,
garlic, khào khùa (ເຂົ້າຂົ້ວ, roast, powdered sticky rice), green
onions, mint leaves and chillies. It can be very hot or rather mild,
depending on the cook or your own request. Làap is typically
served with a large plate of lettuce, mint and steamed mango
leaves. Using your fingers, you wrap a little làap in the lettuce
and herbs and eat it with hand-rolled balls of sticky rice.

beef laap	làap sìin	ລາບຊີ້ນ
chicken laap	làap kai	ລາບໄກ່
fish laap	làap pạa	ລາບປາ
pork laap	làap mǔu	ລາບໝູ

SOUP   ແກງ

fish and lemongrass soup with mushrooms		
tôm yám pạa		ຕົ້ມຍຳປາ
mild soup with vegetables and pork		
kạeng jèut		ແກງຈືດ
same as above, with bean curd		
kạeng jèut tâo-hûu		ແກງຈືດເຕົ້າຮູ້
rice soup with ...	khào pìak ...	ເຂົ້າປຽກ ...
chicken	kai	ໄກ່
fish	pạa	ປາ
pork	mǔu	ໝູ

FOOD

STIR-FRIED DISHES ຂົ້ວ-ອາຫານປະເພດຂົ້ວ

beef in oyster sauce		
ngúa phàt nâm-mán hăwy	ງົວຜັດນ້ຳມັນຫອຍ	
chicken with ginger		
kai phát khǐing	ໄກ່ຜັດຂີງ	
chicken fried with chillies		
kai phát màak phét	ໄກ່ຜັດໝາກເຜັດ	
chicken with mushrooms		
kai phát hét	ໄກ່ຜັດເຫັດ	
stir-fried mixed vegetables		
phát phák	ຜັດຜັກ	
sweet and sour pork		
mǔu sòm-wǎan	ໝູສົ້ມຫວານ	

FISH ປາ

crisp-fried fish	jęun pąa	ຈືນປາ
fried prawns	jęun kûng	ຈືນກຸ້ງ
grilled prawns	pîing kûng	ປີ້ງກຸ້ງ
steamed fish	nèung pąa	ໜຶ່ງປາ
grilled fish	pîing pąa	ປີ້ງປາ
sweet & sour fish	pąa sòm-wǎan	ປາສົ້ມຫວານ
catfish	pąa dúk	ປາດຸກ
carp	pąa pàak	ປາປາກ
eel	ian	ອ່ຽນ
freshwater stingray	pąa fǎa lái	ປາຝາໄລ
giant Mekong catfish	pąa béuk	ປາບຶກ
serpent fish	pąa khaw	ປາຄໍ່
sheatfish	pąa sa-ngúa	ປາສະງົວ

VEGETABLES

ຜັກ

FOOD

bamboo shoots	naw mâi	ໜ່ໄມ້
bean	thua	ຖົ່ວ
bean sprouts	thua ngâwk	ຖົ່ວງອກ
bitter melon	máa-láa-jịin (màak ha)	ມາລາຈິນ (ໝາກຮະ)
cabbage	ká-lam pịi	ກະລ່ຳປີ
cauliflower	ká-lam pịi dàwk	ກະລ່ຳປີດອກ
Chinese radish (daikon)	phák kàat hửa	ຜັກກາດຫົວ
corn	khào săa-líi	ເຂົ້າສາລີ
cucumber	màak tạeng	ໝາກແຕງ
eggplant	màak khểua	ໝາກເຂືອ
garlic	hửa phák thíam	ຫົວຜັກທຽມ
lettuce	phák sá-lat	ຜັກສະລັດ
long green beans	thua nyáo	ຖົ່ວຍາວ
lotus root	tôn bụa	ຕົ້ນບົວ
onion	hửa phák bua	ຫົວຜັກບົ່ວ
onion (green 'scallions')	tôn phák bua	ຕົ້ນຜັກບົ່ວ
peanuts	màak thua dịn	ໝາກຖົ່ວດິນ
potato	mán fa-lang	ມັນຝລັ່ງ
pumpkin	màak éu (màak fák)	ໝາກອື (ໝາກຟັກ)
tomato	màak len	ໝາກເລັ່ນ

WIT & WISDOM

When choosing an elephant, check the tail;
when choosing a wife, look at her mother.

lêuak sang hài boeng hăng,   ເລືອກຊ້າງໃຫ້ເບິ່ງຫາງ
lêuak náan hài boeng mae   ເລືອກນາງໃຫ້ເບິ່ງແມ່

FOOD

CONDIMENTS, HERBS & SPICES

ເຄື່ອງປຸງ, ເຄື່ອງທອມແລະເຄື່ອງເທດ

Along with chillies, lime juice, lemon grass and fresh coriander leaf are added to give Lao food its characteristic tang. Nâm pạa (ນ້ຳປາ), a thin, clear fish sauce made from fermented anchovies, or ká-pí, fermented shrimp paste, provide the cuisine's main salty element.

Other common seasonings include hot chillies, ground peanuts, tamarind juice, lime juice, ginger and coconut milk. Chillies are sometimes served on the side in hot pepper sauces called jaew (ແຈ່ວ).

Granulated salt and ground black pepper are almost never present on a Lao table, although they may be used during the cooking. Soy sauce can be requested, though this is normally used as a condiment for Chinese food only.

chilli	màak phét	ໝາກເຜັດ
coconut extract	nâm ká-thí	ນ້ຳກະທີ
coriander (cilantro)	phák hǎwm	ຜັກຫອມ
dipping sauces	jaew	ແຈ່ວ
dried shrimp	kûng hàeng	ກຸ້ງແຫ້ງ
fish sauce	nâm pạa	ນ້ຳປາ
fish sauce	nâm pạa sai	ນ້ຳປາໃສ່
with chillies	màak phét	ໝາກເຜັດ
ginger	khǐng	ຂີງ
ground peanuts	thua dịn	ຖົ່ວດິນ
lemongrass	hǔa sǒng khái	ຫົວສິງໄຄ
lime juice	nâm màak náo	ນ້ຳໝາກນາວ
salt	kẹua	ເກືອ
sesame	màak ngáa	ໝາກງາ
soy sauce	nâm sá-íu	ນ້ຳສະອິ້ວ
sugar	nâm-tạan	ນ້ຳຕານ
sweet basil	bại hǒh-la-pháa	ໃບໂຫລະພາ
tamarind	màak khǎam	ໝາກຂາມ
vinegar	nâm sòm	ນ້ຳສົ້ມ

COOKING METHODS

ວິທີປຸງແຕ່ງອາຫານ

ອົບ
óp
   baked

ຕົ້ມ
tôm
   boiled

ສຸກ
súk
   cooked/ripe

ແກງ
kạeng
   curried

ຈືນ
jẹun
   fried in large pieces

ຂົ້ວຜັກທຽມຜິກໄທ
khùa phák thíam phik thái
   fried with garlic and black pepper

ຂົ້ວຂີງ
khùa khǐing
   fried with ginger

ປີ້ງ
piing
   grilled, barbecued or roasted

ດິບ
díp
   raw/unripe

ໜຶ່ງ
nèung
   steamed (fish, rice only)

ຂົ້ວ (ຜັດ)
khùa (phát)
   stir-fried or fried in small pieces

FOOD

FRUIT

ໝາກໄມ້

apple (usually imported, year-round)
   màak pọhm

ໝາກໂປມ

banana (year-round)
   màak kûay

ໝາກກ້ວຍ

mandarin orange (year-round)
   màak kîang

ໝາກກ້ຽງ

watermelon (year-round)
   màak móh

ໝາກໂມ

FOOD

TROPICAL DELIGHTS

Laos, like its South-East Asian neighbours, offers travellers an opportunity to indulge in a wide range of tropical fruit – don't miss out!

ໝາກພ້າວ   màak phâo
coconut – grated for cooking when mature, eaten with a spoon when young; juice is sweetest in young coconuts (year-round)

ໝາກຂຽບ   màak khìap
custard-apple (July to October)

ທຸລຽນ   thu-lían
durian – held in high esteem by South-East Asians, but most Westerners dislike this fruit. There are several varieties and seasons, so keep trying.

ໝາກສິດາ   màak sǐi-dạa
guava (year-round)

ໝາກມີ້   màak mîi
jackfruit – similar in outward appearance to durian but much easier to take (year round)

ໝາກນາວ   màak náo
lime (year-round)

ໝາກຍຳໃຍ   màak nyám nyái
longan – 'dragon's eyes', small, brown, spherical, similar to rambutan (July to October)

ໝາກລິ້ນຈີ່   màak lîn-jii
  lychee (July to October)

ໝາກມ່ວງ   màak muang
  mango – several varieties and seasons

ໝາກມັງຄຸດ   màak máng-khut
  mangosteen – round, purple fruit with juicy white flesh
  (April to September)

ໝາກນັດ   màak nat
  pineapple (year-round)

ໝາກຫຸ່ງ   màak hung
  papaya (year-round)

FOOD

ໝາກເຄາະ   màak ngaw
  rambutan – red, hairy-skinned fruit with grape-like
  interior (July to September)

ໝາກກຽງ   màak kiang
  rose-apple – small, apple-like texture, very fragrant
  (April to July)

ອ້ອຍ   âwy
  sugarcane (year round)

ໝາກຂາມ   màak khăam
  tamarind – comes in sweet as well as tart varieties
  (year-round)

FOOD

SWEETS   ເຄື່ອງຫວານ

Restaurant menus rarely offer Lao sweets (ເຄື່ອງຫວານ, kheuang wǎan). Instead the Lao buy these fresh in local morning markets or from street vendors in the evening. Typical ingredients include sticky rice, rice flour, palm and cane sugar, agar-agar (gelatin made from a type of seaweed), shredded coconut, coconut extract, egg yolks and various kinds of fruit.

banana in coconut milk
    nâm wǎan màak kûay   ນ້ຳຫວານໝາກກ້ວຍ

cakes made with sticky rice flour
    khào nǒm   ເຂົ້າໜົມ

custard
    khào sǎng-kha-nyǎa   ສັງຂະຫຍາ

egg custard
    khào-nǒm màw k_ạeng   ເຂົ້າໜົມໝໍ້ແກງ

red sticky rice in coconut cream
    khào nǐaw dạeng   ເຂົ້າໜຽວແດງ

sticky rice in coconut cream and ripe mango
    khào nǐaw màak muang   ເຂົ້າໜຽວໝາກມ່ວງ

sticky rice in coconut milk cooked in bamboo
    khào lǎam   ເຂົ້າຫລາມ

sweetened sticky rice steamed in banana leaves
    khào tôm   ເຂົ້າຕົ້ມ

DRINKS –
NON-ALCOHOLIC
Water

ດື່ມ-
ເຄື່ອງດື່ມທີ່ບໍ່ມີທາດເຫຼົ້າ
ນຳ້

Drinking water (ນຳ້ດື່ມ, nâm deum) is purified for drinking purposes, whether boiled or otherwise treated. All water offered to customers in restaurants or hotels will be purified, so one needn't fret about the safety of taking a sip from a proffered glass or pitcher. In restaurants and most foodstalls, you can order nâm deum by the bottle, or you can ask for drinking water by the glass at no charge. The latter is usually drawn from 20L bottles of purified water or water boiled by the proprietors for drinking purposes.

boiled water	nâm tôm	ນຳ້ຕົ້ມ
drinking water	nâm deum	ນຳ້ດື່ມ
ice	nâm kâwn	ນຳ້ກ້ອນ

FOOD

FOOD

Coffee & Tea   ກາເຟແລະນ້ຳຊາ

Good coffee is grown in the Bolaven Plateau area of Southern Laos. The Lao tend to brew coffee using pure coffee beans (rarely adding ground peanuts or chicory as in Thailand). Traditionally Lao coffee is roasted by wholesalers, ground by vendors and filtered just before serving. The typical Lao restaurant – especially those in hotels, guesthouses and other tourist-oriented establishments – serves instant coffee with packets of artificial, non-dairy creamer on the side.

If you want real Lao coffee ask for kąa-féh thǒng (ກາເຟຖົງ, bag coffee), or ką-féh tôm (ກາເຟຕົ້ມ, boiled coffee), prepared by pouring hot water through a bag-shaped cloth filter containing ground coffee.

The Lao usually serve filtered coffee mixed with sugar. Some shops also add sweetened condensed milk. If you don't want sugar or milk, ask for kąa-féh dạm (ກາເຟດຳ, black coffee) and baw sai nâm-tạan (ບໍ່ໃສ່ນ້ຳຕານ, without sugar). Lao coffee usually comes in a small glass instead of a ceramic cup. Grasp the hot glass along the rim to avoid burnt fingers.

In Central and Southern Laos, coffee is almost always served with a chaser of hot nâm sáa (ນ້ຳຊາ, weak tea), while in the north it's typically served with a glass of plain hot water.

Chinese-style (green or semi-cured) teas predominate in Chinese and Vietnamese restaurants and are always served plain, ie, without sugar or milk. Black, Indian-style tea is typically found only in restaurants or foodstalls that serve Lao coffee. If you order sáa hâwn (ຊາຮ້ອນ, hot tea), it may arrive with sugar and condensed milk, so be sure to specify sáa dạm baw sai nâm-tạan (ຊາດຳບໍ່ໃສ່ນ້ຳຕານ) if you prefer black tea without milk and/or sugar.

FOOD

hot water	nâm hâwn	ນ້ຳຮ້ອນ
cold water	nâm yén	ນ້ຳເຢັນ
hot Lao coffee with milk and sugar	kạa-féh nóm hâwn	ກາເຟນົມຮ້ອນ
hot Lao coffee with sugar, no milk	kạa-féh dạm	ກາເຟດຳ
hot Nescafé with milk and sugar	naet nóm	ແນດນົມ
hot Nescafé with sugar, no milk	naet dạm	ແນດດຳ
iced Lao coffee with sugar, no milk	kạa-féh nóm yén	ກາເຟນົມເຢັນ
iced Lao coffee with milk and sugar	òh-lîang	ໂອລ້ຽງ
weak tea	nâm sáa	ນ້ຳຊາ
hot Lao tea with sugar	sáa hâwn	ຊາຮ້ອນ
hot Lao tea with milk and sugar	sáa nóm hâwn	ຊານົມຮ້ອນ
iced Lao tea with milk and sugar	sáa nóm yén	ຊານົມເຢັນ
iced Lao tea with sugar, no milk	sáa wăan yén	ຊາຫວານເຢັນ
no sugar	baw sai nâm-tạan	ບໍ່ໃສ່ນ້ຳຕານ
Ovaltine	oh-wan-tin	ໂອວັນຕິນ
orange juice (or orange soda)	nâm màak kîang	ນ້ຳຫມາກກ້ຽງ
plain milk	nâm nóm	ນ້ຳນົມ
yogurt	nóm sòm	ນົມສົ້ມ

DRINKS – ALCOHOLIC
ດື່ມ-ເຫຼົ້າ
Beer
ເບຍ

Several kinds of beer are brewed by the Lao Brewery Company on the outskirts of Vientiane. Least expensive but very drinkable is LBC's draft beer (ເບຍສົດ, bịa sòt), which is only available in beer bars in Vientiane. LBC also bottles a Bia Lao (the French label reads Bière Larue) – look for the tiger's head on the label. In the northern provinces bordering China, various Chinese brands of beer are available – these generally cost less than Lao beer.

Distilled Spirits
ເຫຼົ້າ

Rice whisky or lào láo (ເຫຼົ້າລາວ, Lao liquor) is a popular drink among lowland Lao. The government produces several brands which are very similar in taste to Thailand's famous 'Mekong whisky' and are best taken over ice with a splash of soda and a squeeze of lime.

In rural provinces, a weaker version of lào láo is fermented by households or villages. Strictly speaking, it's not legal but no-one seems to care. It's not always safe to drink, however, since unboiled water is often added during and after the fermentation process.

beer	bịa	ເບຍ
draught beer	bịa sót	ເບຍສົດ
Lao rice whisky	lào láo	ເຫຼົ້າລາວ
soda water	nâm sŏh-dạa	ນ້ຳໂສດາ
glass	jàwk	ຈອກ
bottle	kâew	ແກ້ວ

WEATHER

ອາກາດ

How's the weather?
ąa-káat pęn jang-dąi

ອາກາດເປັນຈັ່ງໃດ

The weather is nice today.
mêu-nîi ąa-kàat dịi

ມື້ນີ້ອາກາດດີ

The weather isn't good.
ąa-kàat baw dịi

ອາກາດບໍ່ດີ

Is it going to rain?
fǒn sii tók lěu baw

ຝົນຊິຕົກຫລືບໍ່

It's ...

windy	lóm phat	ລົມພັດ
not windy	lóm baw phat	ລົມບໍ່ພັດ
very cold	nǎo lǎai	ໜາວຫລາຍ
very hot	hâwn lǎai	ຮ້ອນຫລາຍ
raining hard	fǒn tók nak	ຝົນຕົກໜັກ
flooding	nám thûam	ນ້ຳຖ້ວມ
cool weather	ąa-kàat yęn	ອາກາດເຢັນ
hot weather	ąa-kàat hâwn	ອາກາດຮ້ອນ
fog	nâm màwk	ນ້ຳໝອກ
lightning	fâa mâep	ຟ້າແມບ
monsoon	máw-la-sǔm	ມໍລະສຸມ
weather	ąa-kàat	ອາກາດ

TREKKING

ການເດີນປ່າ

Are there guided treks?
míi pha-nak-ngáan nám thiaw
baw dǫen paa

ມີພະນັກງານ
ນຳທ່ຽວບໍ່ເດີນປ່າ

Do we need a guide?
jąm pęn tâwng míi
pha-nak-ngáan nám thiaw baw

ຈຳເປັນຕ້ອງມີ ພະນັກງານ
ນຳທ່ຽວ

Does the price include ...?	láa-kháa huam nám khaa ... baw	ລາຄາຮ່ວມ ນຳຄ່າ ... ບໍ
food	aa-hǎan	ອາຫານ
transport	khǒn-song	ຂົນສົ່ງ

How many hours per day will we walk?
já nyaang mêu-la ják
sua-móhng
ຈະຍ່າງມື້ລະຈັກ
ຊົ່ວໂມງ

Is it a difficult walk?
tháang pai nyâak baw
ທາງໄປຫຍາກບໍ່

I/We would like to hire a guide.
yàak jâang pha-nak-ngáan
nám thiaw
ຍາກຈ້າງ
ພະນັກງານນຳທ່ຽວ

backpack	baa-lóh/thǒng pêh	ບາໂລ/ຖົງເປ້
compass	khěm thit	ເຂັມທິດ
first-aid kit	thǒng yáa pá-jaam baan	ຖົງຢາປະຈຳບ້ານ
guide (person)	pha-nak-ngáan nám thiaw	ພະນັກງານ ນຳທ່ຽວ
guided trek	pha-nak ngáan nám thiaw dออn paa	ພະນັກງານນຳ ທ່ຽວເດີນປ່າ
hiking boots	kòep doen paa	ເກີບເດີນປ່າ
map	phǎen-thii	ແຜນທີ່
mountain climbing	kaan pin phúu	ການປີນພູ
provisions	kheuang doen paa	ເຄື່ອງເດີນປ່າ
rope	sêuak	ເຊືອກ
signpost	pâai bàwk tháang	ປ້າຍບອກທາງ
tour/trek	thawng thiaw; doen paa	ທ່ອງທ່ຽວ/ເດີນປ່າ
to walk	nyaang	ຍ່າງ

Where is the trail to ...?
tháang pai ... yuu sǎi
ທາງໄປ ... ຢູ່ໃສ

Which is the shortest route?
tháang dai sàn kwaa
ທາງໃດສັ້ນກວ່າ

Which is the easiest route?
tháang dai sá-dùak kwaa
ທາງໃດສະດວກກວ່າ

Where's the nearest village?
  muu bâan thii yuu kâi   ໝູ່ບ້ານທີ່ໃກ້
  kwaa muu sǎi   ກ່ວາໝູ່ຢູ່ໃສ

Is it safe to climb this mountain?
  khêun phuu nîi pàwt phái baw   ຂຶ້ນພູນີ້ປອດໄພບໍ່

Is there a hut up there?
  yuu thóeng phúu míi thǐang   ຢູ່ເທິງພູມີຕຽງໄຫບໍ່
  hai baw

I'd like to talk to someone who
knows this area.
  yàak lóm káp phûu hûu   ຢາກລົມກັບຜູ້ຮູ້ພື້ນທີ່ນີ້
  phêun thii nîi

How far is it from ... to ...?
  tae ... thǒeng ... kai thao dai   ແຕ່ ... ເຖິງ ... ໄກເທົ່າໃດ

Where have you come from?
  jâo máa tae sǎi   ເຈົ້າມາແຕ່ໃສ

How long did it take you?
  jâo sâi wéh-láa lǎai   ເຈົ້າໃຊ້ເວລາຫລາຍ
  paan dai   ປານໃດ

How many ...?	ják ...	ຈັກ ...
days	mêu	ມື້
hours	sua-móhng	ຊົ່ວໂມງ
kilometres	kí-lóh-maet	ກິໂລແມັດ
metres	maet	ແມັດ

IN THE COUNTRY

DID YOU KNOW ... From its source on the Tibetan
Plateau, the Mekong River
passes through Yunnan,
then into Laos and Thailand,
dropping by Cambodia
before entering the South
China Sea through its delta
in Vietnam – it is the 12th
longest river in the world.

IN THE COUNTRY

I'm lost.
   khàwy lŏng tháang   ຂ້ອຍຫລົງທາງ
Does this path go to ...?
   tháang nîi pai hâwt ...   ທາງນີ້ໄປຮອດ ...
How long is the trail?
   tháang nyáo paan dại   ທາງຍາວປານໃດ
Is the track well-marked?
   míi pâai bàwk tháang baw   ມີປ້າຍບອກທາງບໍ່
Can we go through here?
   phaan tháang nîi dâi baw   ຜ່ານທາງນີ້ໄດ້ບໍ່
When does it get dark?
   ják móhng sii mêut   ຈັກໂມງຊິມືດ
Where can we buy supplies?
   sêu kheuang sâi dâi yuu săi ຊື້ເຄື່ອງໃຊ້ໄດ້ຢູ່ໃສ
Who lives here?
   phăi yuu bawn nîi   ໃຜຢູ່ບ່ອນນີ້
Can I/we stay in this village?
   khàwy/phǔak háo phak   ຂ້ອຍ/ພວກເຮົາພັກ
   yuu bâan nîi dâi baw   ຢູ່ບ້ານນີ້ໄດ້ບໍ່
Can I/we sleep here?
   khàwy/phǔak háo náwn   ຂ້ອຍ/ພວກເຮົານອນ
   yuu nîi dâi baw   ຢູ່ນີ້ໄດ້ບໍ່

blanket	phàa hom	ຜ້າຫົ່ມ
hill tribe (High Lao)	sáo khăo	ຊາວເຂົາ
lodging	bawn phak	ບ່ອນພັກ
medicine	yạa	ຢາ
mosquitoes	nyúng	ຍຸງ
mosquito coil	yạa jút kạn nyúng	ຢາຈຸດກັນຍຸງ
mosquito net	mûng	ມຸ້ງ
opium	yạa fín	ຢາຝິ່ນ
raft	pháe	ແພ
village headman	nai bâan	ນາຍບ້ານ
water	nâm	ນ້ຳ

CAMPING

ການຕັ້ງຄ້າຍ

In general, the Lao government permits foreigners to camp outdoors only when they are participating in a tour led by a Lao PDR-licensed tour agency. This may change as Laos opens further to tourism.

camping	ķaan tâng khêm	ການຕັ້ງເຄ້ມ
campsite	bawn tâng khêm	ບ່ອນຕັ້ງເຄ້ມ
rope	sêuak	ເຊືອກ
sleeping bag	thŏng náwn	ຖົງນອນ
tent	tùup phàa	ຕູບຜ້າ
torch (flashlight)	fái sǎai	ໄຟສາຍ

Is there a campsite nearby?
  yuu kâi nîi míi bawn tâng
  khêm baw

ຢູ່ໃກ້ນີ້ມີບ່ອນຕັ້ງເຄ້ມບໍ່

Where's the nearest campsite?
  bawn tâng khêm thii
  kâi thii sút yuu sǎi

ບ່ອນຕັ້ງເຄ້ມທີ່ໃກ້
ທີ່ສຸດຢູ່ໃສ

Is drinking water available?
  míi nâm deum baw

ມີນ້ຳດື່ມບໍ່

Can I/we put a tent here?
  [khàwy; phûak háo] tâng
  tùup phàa yuu nîi dâi baw

ຂ້ອຍ; ພວກເຮົາ ຕັ້ງ
ຕູບຜ້າຢູ່ນີ້ໄດ້ບໍ່

Is it safe?
  pàwt phái baw

ປອດໄພບໍ່

Is drinking water available?
  míi nâm deum baw

ມີນ້ຳດື່ມບໍ່

CYCLING   ການຂີ່ລົດຖີບ

Bicycles are a popular form of transport throughout urban Laos and can be hired cheaply almost anywhere there are guesthouses. These Thai- or Chinese-made street bikes come in varying degrees of usability, so be sure to inspect the bikes thoroughly before renting. Lao customs doesn't object to visitors bringing bicycles into the country.

Where can I hire a bike?
khàwy já sao lot thìip
dâi yuu săi
ຂ້ອຍຈະເຊົ່າລົດ
ຖີບໄດ້ຢູ່ໃສ

How much is it for ...?	khaa sao thao dǎai taw ...	ຄ່າເຊົ່າເທົ່າ ໃດຕໍ່ ...
an hour	neung sua-móhng	ໜຶ່ງຊົ່ວໂມງ
the morning	tạwn sào	ຕອນເຊົ້າ
the afternoon	tạwn baai	ຕອນບ່າຍ
the day	neung wan	ໜຶ່ງວັນ

Where can I find second-hand
bikes for sale?
míi lot thìip méu săwng
khǎai yuu săi
ມີລົດຖີບມືສອງຂາຍຢູ່ໃສ

Is it within cycling distance?
tháang nǐi pẹn wóng jawn
săm-láp khii lot thìip baw
ທາງນີ້ເປັນວົງຈອນ
ສຳລັບຂີ່ລົດຖີບບໍ່

Is the trail suitable for bikes?
tháang nǐi máw săm-láp
khii lot thìip baw
ທາງນີ້ເໝາະ
ສຳລັບຂີ່ລົດຖີບບໍ່

I have a flat tyre.
tịin lot khàwy hua
ຕີນລົດຂ້ອຍຮົ່ວ

bicycle	lot thìip	ລົດຖີບ
brakes	hàam	ຫ້າມ
to cycle	thìip	ຖີບ
gear stick	khan kịa	ຄັນເກຍ

handlebars	khǎo	ເຂົາ
helmet	mùak kạn nawk	ໝວກກັນນ໊ອກ
inner tube	yáang nái	ຍາງໃນ
lights	fái tạa	ໄຟຕາ
padlock	ká-jae	ກະແຈ
pump	kâwng sùup	ກ້ອງສູບ
puncture	hua	ຮົວ
saddle	ạan	ອານ
wheel	kọng lot	ກົງລົດ

IN THE COUNTRY

GEOGRAPHY   ພູມມິສາດ

Many town and village names in Laos incorporate the following geographic or demographic features.

Ban or Baan (village)	bâan	ບ້ານ
Don (river island)	dạwn	ດອນ
Khok or Kok (knoll or mound)	khóhk	ໂຄກ
Muang (city or district)	méuang	ເມື້ອງ
Nakhon (large city)	na-kháwn	ນະຄອນ
Nam (river in Northern Laos)	nâm	ນ້ຳ
Non (hill, knoll or mound)	nóhn	ໂນນ
Nong (pond/lake)	nǎwng	ໜອງ
Pak (mouth – usually at a river mouth)	pàak	ປາກ
Se (rivers in Southern Laos)	séh	ເຊ
Vieng (city)	wíang	ວຽງ
Xieng (city)	síang	ຊຽງ

IN THE COUNTRY

A POTTED HISTORY

PLAIN OF JARS   ທົ່ງໄຫຫິນ

Among the most enigmatic sights in Laos are several meadow-like areas in Xieng Khuang Province littered with large stone jars. Quite a few theories have been advanced as to the functions of the stone jars – that they were used as sarcophagi, as wine fermenters or for rice storage – but the most likely theory suggests they held relics associated with ritual reburial. White quartzite rocks have also been found lying next to some of the jars, along with vases that may have contained human remains.

Aerial photographic evidence suggests that a thin 'track' of jars may link the various jar sites in Xieng Khuang, and some researchers hope future excavations will uncover sealed jars whose contents may be relatively intact.

The jars are commonly said to be 2000 years old, but in the absence of any organic material associated with the jars – eg, bones or food remains – there's no reliable way to date them. The jars may be associated with the equally mysterious stone megaliths found off Route 6 on the way north to Sam Neua, and/or with large Dongson drum-shaped stone objects discovered in Luang Prabang Province. All of the unanswered questions regarding the Plain of Jars (thong hải hǐn) make this area ripe for archaeological investigation, a proceeding that has been slowed by years of war and by the presence of UXO (unexploded ordnance).

Site 1, 15km south-west of Phonsavan and the largest of the various sites, features 250 jars which weigh from 600kg to one tonne each; the biggest of them weighs as much as six tonnes. The jars have been fashioned from solid stone, most from a tertiary conglomerate known as molasses, akin to sandstone, and a few from granite.

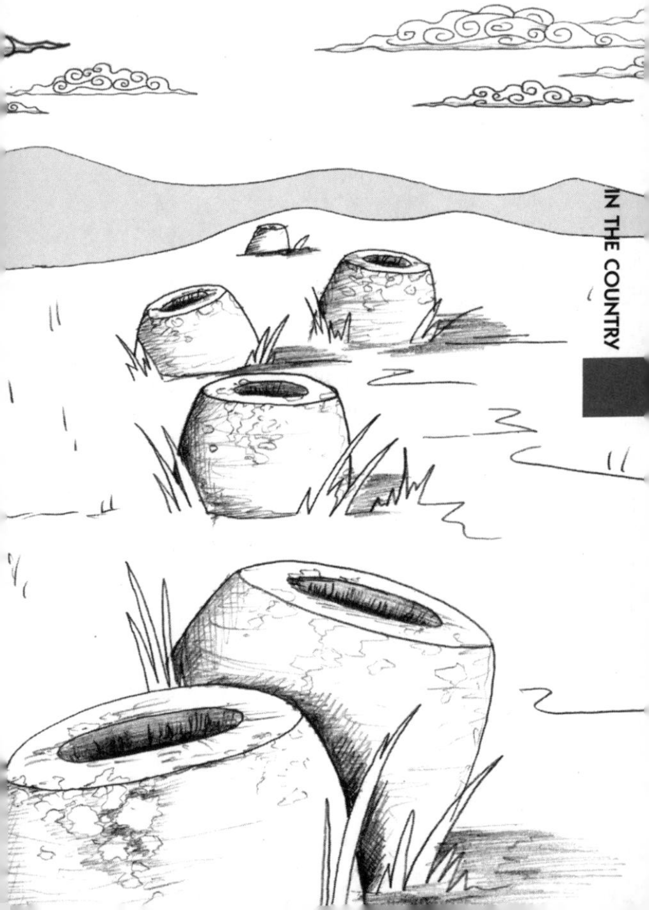

IN THE COUNTRY

GEOGRAPHIC FEATURES ພູມມິປະເທດອື່ນ

cave	thàm	ຖ້ຳ
cliff	phǎa	ຜາ
countryside	bâan nâwk	ບ້ານນອກ
field (dry)	hai	ໄຮ່
footpath	tháang nyaang	ທາງຍ່າງ
forest	paa	ປ່າ
hill	phúu nâwy	ພູນ້ອຍ
jungle	dong	ດົງ
mountain	phúu khǎo	ພູເຂົາ
mountain peak	jawm phúu	ຈອມພູ
nature	thám-ma-sâat	ທຳມະຊາດ
rice field (wet)	náa	ນາ
river	nâm	ນ້ຳ
riverbank	fang nâm	ຝັ່ງນ້ຳ
river rapids	kâeng	ແກ້ງ
sea	tha-léh	ທະເລ
spring/well	baw nâm	ບໍ່ນ້ຳ
stone	hǐn	ຫິນ
stream	hùay	ຫ້ວຍ
swamp	bẹung	ບຶງ
trail	tháang thiaw	ທາງທ່ຽວ
waterfall	nâm tók tàat	ນ້ຳຕົກຕາດ

ANIMALS ສັດປ່າ

ant	mót	ມົດ
banteng (type of wild cattle)	ngúa dàeng	ງົວແດງ
barking deer	fáan	ຟານ
bear	mǐi	ໝີ
bee	mae phòeng	ແມ່ເຜິ້ງ
bird	nok	ນົກ
butterfly	máeng ká-bêua	ແມງກະເບື້ອ

civet	ngǐan	ເຫງັນ
cockroach	máeng sàap	ແມງສາບ
cow	ngúa	ງົວ
crocodile	khàe	ແຂ້
deer	kwạang	ກວາງ
dog	mǎa	ໝາ
dolphin	pạa lóh-máa	ປາໂລມາ
duck	pét	ເປັດ
elephant	sâang	ຊ້າງ
fish	pạa	ປາ
fishing cat	sěua pạa	ເສືອປາ
fly	máeng wán	ແມງວັນ
frog	kóp	ກົບ
gaur	ká-thíng	ກະທິງ
gecko	káp-kâe	ກັບແກ້
gibbon	sa-níi	ຊະນີ
horse	mǎa	ມ້າ
leaf monkey	khaang	ຄ່າງ
leopard	sěua dạo	ເສືອດາວ
monkey	líng	ລິງ
rabbit	ká-tại	ກະຕ່າຍ
rhinoceros	hâet	ແຮດ
scorpion	máeng ngáo	ແມງເງົາ
shrimp	kûng	ກຸ້ງ
snake	ngúu	ງູ
snake (venomous)	ngúu phít	ງູພິດ
tiger	sěua khong	ເສືອໂຄ່ງ
turtle	tao	ເຕົ່າ
water buffalo	khu-wáai	ຄວາຍ
water fowl	nok nâm	ນົກນ້ຳ
wild animals	sát paa	ສັດປ່າ
wild buffalo	khuáai paa	ຄວາຍປ່າ
young animal; offspring	lûuk sát	ລູກສັດ

PLANTS

ຕົ້ນ

bamboo	phai	ໄຜ່
dipterocarp	yáang	ຍາງ
flower	dàwk mâi	ດອກໄມ້
grass/herb	nyàa	ຫຍ້າ
pine	tôn sǒn	ຕົ້ນສົນ
tree	tôn mâi	ຕົ້ນໄມ້
teak	tôn sák	ຕົ້ນສັກ

IN THE COUNTRY

DID YOU KNOW ... The *dipterocarp* is a member of a family of evergreen trees commonly found in south Asia and Africa, named for its helicopter-like seed pods. It's generally a large tree, known for its leathery leaves and aromatic resins. The tree can be used as a source of timber and in the production of varnishes and herbal remedies.

I need a ...	khàwy tâwng-kạan ...	ຂ້ອຍຕ້ອງການ ...
dentist	mǎw pụa khàew	ໝໍປົວແຂ້ວ
doctor	thaan mǎw	ທ່ານໝໍ

Where's the nearest ...?	... yùu sǎi	... ຢູ່ໃສ
chemist	khóm bụng yáa	ຄົມບຸງຢາ
hospital	hóhng mǎw	ໂຮງໝໍ

I'm sick.
khàwy baw sá-bại

ຂ້ອຍບໍ່ສະບາຍ

My friend is sick.
pheuan khàwy baw sá-bại

ເພື່ອນຂ້ອຍບໍ່ສະບາຍ

I need a doctor who speaks English.
khàwy tâwng-kạan thaan
mǎw hûu pháa-sǎa ạng-kít

ຂ້ອຍຕ້ອງການທ່ານ
ໝໍຮູ້ພາສາອັງກິດ

Could the doctor come here?
thaan mǎw máa nîi dâi baw

ທ່ານໝໍມານີ້ໄດ້ບໍ່

WOMEN'S HEALTH

ສຸຂະພາບແມ່ຍິງ

Could I see a female doctor?
khàwy khǎw phop thaan
mǎw phùu nýíng dâi baw

ຂ້ອຍຂໍພົບທ່ານ
ໝໍຜູ້ຍິງໄດ້ບໍ່

I'm pregnant.
khàwy thěu pháa-máan

ຂ້ອຍຖືພາມານ

I'm on the Pill.
khàwy kịn yáa khúm

ຂ້ອຍກິນຍາຄຸມ

I haven't had my period for ... weeks.
pá-jạm dẹuan khàwy baw
máa dâi ... ạa-thit lâew

ປະຈຳເດືອນຂ້ອຍບໍ່
ມາໄດ້ ... ອາທິດແລ້ວ

AILMENTS

ການເຈັບເປັນ

I'm tired.	khàwy meuay	ຂ້ອຍເໝື່ອຍ
I'm not well.	khàwy baw sá-bąai	ຂ້ອຍບໍ່ສະບາຍ
I have a cold.	pęn wát	ເປັນຫວັດ
I have a fever.	pęn khài	ເປັນໄຂ້
My stomach aches.	pùat thâwng	ປວດທ້ອງ
I have diarrhoea.	lóng thâwng	ລົງທ້ອງ
It hurts here.	jép yuu níi	ເຈັບຢູ່ນີ້
I can't sleep.	náwn baw lap	ນອນບໍ່ລັບ
My head aches.	pùat hǔa	ປວດຫົວ
My back hurts.	pùat lǎng	ປວດຫຼັງ

There's pain in my chest.
  jép nàa óek
  ເຈັບໜ້າເອິກ

I have a sore throat.
  jép kháw
  ເຈັບຄໍ

I have vomited several times.
  hàak lǎai theua
  ຮາກຫຼາຍເທື່ອ

I have been like this for two weeks.
  pęn naew níi dai sǎwng
  ເປັນແນວນີ້ໄດ້ສອງ
  ąa-thit lâew
  ອາທິດແລ້ວ

Is it serious?
  pęn nák baw
  ເປັນໜັກບໍ່

I feel ...	khàwy hûu-séuk ...	ຂ້ອຍຮູ້ສຶກ ...
dizzy	įn hua	ວິນຫົວ
shivery	nǎo son	ໜາວສັ່ນ
weak	awn phía	ອ່ອນເພຍ

ache	pùat	ປວດ
AIDS	lôhk èht	ໂລກເອດສ
allergy	phâe	ແພ້
anaemia	lôhk lêuat jąang	ໂລກເລືອດຈາງ
asthma	lôhk hèut	ໂລກຫືດ
blister	pęn tum	ເປັນຕຸ່ມ

bronchitis	làwt lóm ák-sèhp	ຫລອດລົມອັກເສບ
burn	fái mâi	ໄຟໄໝ້
cancer	ma-léhng	ມະເລງ
cholera	a-hí-wáa	ອະຫິວາ
cough	ại	ໄອ
cramps	pân (phùuk)	ປັ້ນ (ຜູກ)
dengue fever	khài lêuat àwk	ໄຂ້ເລືອດອອກ
diabetes	lôhk bạo wǎan	ໂລກເບົາຫວານ
diarrhoea	lóng thâwng	ລົງທ້ອງ
dysentery	lôhk thâwng bít	ໂລກທ້ອງບິດ
fever	khài	ໄຂ້
headache	pùat hǔa	ປວດຫົວ
heart condition	sá-phâap hǔa jại	ສະພາບຫົວໃຈ
hepatitis	tàp ák-sèhp	ຕັບອັກເສບ
infection	séum sêua	ຊຶມເຊື້ອ

inflammation	ák-sèhp	ອັກເສບ
influenza	khài wát nyai	ໄຂ້ຫວັດໃຫຍ່
lice	tọh hǎo	ໂຕເຫົາ
malaria	khài yúng	ໄຂ້ຍຸງ
migraine	jep hǔa háeng	ເຈັບຫົວແຮງ
pneumonia	lôhk pàwt bụam	ໂລກປອດບວມ
rabies	lôhk pẹn wâw	ໂລກເປັນວໍ້
rash	tum	ຕຸ່ມ
sore throat	jep kháw	ເຈັບຄໍ
sprain	pùat khat	ປວດຂັດ
stomachache	pùat thâwng	ປວດທ້ອງ
sunburn	mâi dàet	ໄໝ້ແດດ
toothache	jép khàew	ເຈັບແຂ້ວ
veneral disease	kạm-ma lôhk	ກຳມະໂລກ

HEALTH

THEY MAY SAY ...

pęn nyǎng	ເປັນຫຍັງ
What's the matter?	
jâo jép nyǎng baw	ເຈົ້າເຈັບຫຍັງບໍ່
Do you feel any pain?	
jép yuu sǎi	ເຈັບຢູ່ໃສ
Where does it hurt?	
pęn bàep nǐi dǫn	ເປັນແບບນີ້ດົນ
bạan-dại lâew	ປານໃດແລ້ວ
How long have you	
been like this?	
jâo khóei pęn bǎep nǐi baw	ເຈົ້າເຄີຍເປັນແບບນີ້ບໍ່
Have you had this before?	
jâo kịn yáa baw	ເຈົ້າກິນຢາບໍ່
Are you on medication?	
jâo phâe ạn-dại baw	ເຈົ້າແພ້ອັນໃດບໍ່
Are you allergic to anything?	
jâo thěu pháa-máan baw	ເຈົ້າຖືພາມານບໍ່
Are you pregnant?	

PARTS OF THE BODY   ພາກສ່ວນຂອງຮ່າງກາຍ

arm	khǎen	ແຂນ
back	lǎng	ຫລັງ
breast	tâo nóm	ເຕົ້ານົມ
chest	óek	ເອິກ
ear	hǔu	ຫູ
eye	tạa	ຕາ
face	nàa	ໜ້າ
finger	nîu méu	ນິ້ວມື
foot/feet	tịin	ຕີນ
hand	méu	ມື
head	hǔa	ຫົວ
heart	hǔa jai	ຫົວໃຈ
jaw	kháang ká-tại	ຄາງກະໄຕ

HEALTH

kidney	màak khai lăng	ໝາກໄຂ່ຫລັງ
knee	hŭa khao	ຫົວເຂົ່າ
leg	khăa	ຂາ
liver	táp	ຕັບ
lungs	pàwt	ປອດ
mouth	pàak	ປາກ
muscle	kâam sîin	ກ້າມຊີ້ນ
nose	dang	ດັງ
penis	a-wái-ya-wa	ອະໄວຍະວະ
	phêht sáai	ເພດຊາຍ
ribs	ká-dùuk khàang	ກະດູກຂ້າງ
shoulders	baa-lai	ບ່າໄລ່
spine	ká-dùuk săn lăng	ກະດູກສັນຫລັງ
stomach	thâwng (ká-phaw)	ທ້ອງ (ກະເພາະ)
testicles	an-tha (hăm)	ອັນທະ (ຫຳ)
throat	kháw	ຄໍ
toe	nîu tjin	ນິ້ວຕີນ
tooth/teeth	khàew	ແຂ້ວ
vagina	sâwng khâwt	ຊ່ອງຄອດ

AT THE CHEMIST   ຢູ່ຮ້ານຂາຍຢາ

antibiotics	yáa tâan sêua	ຢາຕ້ານເຊື້ອ
	(sa-nit kin)	(ຊະນິດກິນ)
antiseptic	yáa tâan sêua	ຢາຕ້ານເຊື້ອ
	(sa-nit tháa)	(ຊະນິດທາ)
aspirin	àet-sá-pęh-lín	ແອສເປລິນ
Band-Aid (plaster)	phàa tít bàat	ຜ້າຕິດບາດ
bandage	phàa haw bàat	ຜ້າຫໍ່ບາດ
condom (latex)	thŏng yang á-náa-mái	ຖົງຢາງອະນາໄມ
gauze	phàa kâw	ຜ້າກໍ້
injection	sák yạa	ສັກຢາ
insulin	yạa kâe lôhk	ຢາແກ້ໂລກ
	bạo wăan	ເບົາຫວານ

morphine	máw-fíin	ມໍຟີນ
painkiller	yạa kâe pùat	ຍາແກ້ປວດ
pill/tablet	yạ met	ຍາເມັດ
prescription	bại sang yạa	ໃບສັ່ງຢາ
sleeping medication	yạa náwn láp	ຍານອນລັບ
vitamin	wi-tạa-mín	ວິຕາມິນ

I need something for ...
   khàwy tâwng-kạan ạn-dại ຂ້ອຍຕ້ອງການອັນໃດ
   ạn neung pheua ... ອັນໜຶ່ງເພື່ອ ...
I have a prescription.
   khàwy míi bại sang yáa ຂ້ອຍມີໃບສັ່ງຢາ
How many times a day?
   mêu-la ják theua ມື້ລະຈັກເທື່ອ
(Four) times a day.
   mêu-la (sii) theua ມື້ລະ (ສີ່) ເທື່ອ
How much per tablet/pill?
   láa kháa met-la thao dại ລາຄາເມັດລະເທົ່າໃດ

Useful Words   ຄຳສັບທີ່ເປັນປະໂຫຍດ

accident	ú-bát-tí-hèht	ອຸບັດຕິເຫດ
addict	khón tít yạa	ຄົນຕິດຢາ
allergic (to)	phâe	ແພ້
ambulance	lot hóhng mǎw	ລົດໂຮງໝໍ
bite	kát	ກັດ
blood test	kùat lêuat	ກວດເລືອດ
blood	lêuat	ເລືອດ
bone	ká-dùuk	ກະດູກ
faint	pẹn lóm	ເປັນລົມ
hospital	hóhng mǎw	ໂຮງໝໍ
ill	puay	ປ່ວຍ
inject	sák yáa	ສັກຢາ

HEALTH

itch	khán	ถັม
mentally ill	sǐa jít	ເສຍຈິດ
nurse	náang pha-yáa-bạan	ນາງພະຍາບານ
pain	khwáam jép-pùat	ຄວາມເຈັບປວດ
patient (n)	khón jép	ຄົນເຈັບ
pharmacy	hâan khǎai yạa	ຮ້ານຂາຍຢາ
pregnant	thěu pháa-máan	ຖືພາມານ
skin	phǐu nǎng	ຜິວໜັງ
vitamins	wi-tạa-mín	ວິຕາມິນ
wound	bàat phǎe (baat jép)	ບາດແຜ (ບາດເຈັບ)

I feel better/worse.
    khàwy hûu-séuk dịi khêun/   ຂ້ອຍຮູ້ສຶກດີຂຶ້ນ/
    jép-kwaa kao   ເຈັບກ່ວາເກົ່າ

I've been vaccinated.
    khàwy dâi sák yáa pâwng   ຂ້ອຍໄດ້ສັກຢາປ້ອງ
    kạn lâew   ກັນແລ້ວ

I have high/low blood pressure.
    khàwy míi khwáam dạn   ຂ້ອຍມີຄວາມດັນ
    lêuat sǔung/tam   ເລືອດສູງ/ຕ່ຳ

I have my own syringe.
    khàwy míi sá-léng   ຂ້ອຍມີສະແລ້ງສັກຢາ
    sak yáa suan tua   ສ່ວນຕົວ

I'm ...	khàwy pẹn ...	ຂ້ອຍເປັນ ...
diabetic	lôhk bạo wǎn	ໂລກເບົາຫວານ
asthmatic	lôhk héut	ໂລກຫຶດ
anaemic	lôhk lêuat jạang	ໂລກເລືອດຈາງ

I'm allergic to ...	khàwy phâe ...	ຂ້ອຍແພ້ ...
antibiotics	yáa tâan sêua	ຢາຕ້ານເຊື້ອ
aspirin	áet-sá-pẹh-lín	ແອສເປລິນ
penicillin	pẹh-níi-síi-lín	ເປນິຊິລິນ

HEALTH

AT THE DENTIST

ຍູ່ທັນຕະແພດ

I have a toothache.
khàwy jép khàew

ຂ້ອຍເຈັບແຂ້ວ

I have a cavity.
khàwy pẹn khàew máeng

ຂ້ອຍເປັນແຂ້ວແມງ

I need a filling.
khàwy tâwng-kạan át khàew

ຂ້ອຍຕ້ອງການອັດແຂ້ວ

I've broken my tooth.
khàew khàwy tàek

ແຂ້ວຂ້ອຍແຕກ

My gums hurt.
khàwy jép hèuak

ຂ້ອຍເຈັບເຫືອກ

I don't want it extracted.
khàwy baw yàak lok khàew

ຂ້ອຍບໍ່ຢາກລົກແຂ້ວ

Please give me an anaesthetic.
suay sai yáa méun hài dae

ຊ່ວຍໃສ່ຍາມຶນໃຫ້ແດ່

| Ouch! | ọhy | ໂອຍ |

SPECIFIC NEEDS

DISABLED TRAVELLERS

ນັກທ່ອງທ່ຽວພິການ

I'm disabled.
khàwy pẹn khón phi-kạan

ຂ້ອຍເປັນຄົນພິການ

I need assistance.
khàwy tâwng-kạan khwáam
suay lěua

ຂ້ອຍຕ້ອງການຄວາມ
ຊ່ວຍເຫລືອ

What services do you have
for disabled people?
jào bạw-li-kạan nyǎng dae
sǎm-láp khón phi-kạan

ເຈົ້າບໍລິການຫຍັງແດ່
ສຳລັບຄົນພິການ

Is there wheelchair access?
kạo-îi lâw kháo pại dâi baw

ເກົ້າອີ້ລໍ້ເຂົ້າໄປໄດ້ບໍ່

Can you bring me a wheelchair?
jào ạo kạo-îi lâw
máa hạp khàwy dâi baw

ເຈົ້າເອົາເກົ້າອີ້ລໍ້
ມາຮັບຂ້ອຍໄດ້ບໍ່

I'm deaf.
khàwy hǔu nùak

ຂ້ອຍຫູໜວກ

I have a hearing aid.
khàwy míi kheuang suay fáng

ຂ້ອຍມີເຄື່ອງຊ່ວຍຟັງ

Speak more loudly, please.
ká-lu-náa wào
dạng-dạng dae

ກະລຸນາເວົ້າດັງໆແດ່

Are guide dogs permitted?
mǎa suay khon tạa
bàwt á-nu-nyâat baw

ໝາຊ່ວຍຄົນຕາບອດ
ອະນຸຍາດບໍ່

disabled person	khón phi-kạan	ຄົນພິການ
guide dog	mǎa suay	ໝາຊ່ວຍ
	khón tạa bàwt	ຄົນຕາບອດ
wheelchair	kạo îi lâw	ເກົ້າອີ້ລໍ້

TRAVELLING WITH THE FAMILY

ເດີນທາງກັບຄອບຄົວ

Are there facilities for babies?
    míi sing ạm-núay khwáam
    sá-dùak sǎm-láp dék baw

ມີສິ່ງອຳນວຍຄວາມ
ສະດວກສຳລັບເດັກບໍ່

Do you have a child-minding service?
    míi bạw-li-kạan dụu láe
    dék nâwy baw

ມີບໍລິການດູ
ແລເດັກນ້ອຍບໍ່

Where can I find a ... -speaking babysitter? [insert country name from page 50]
    khàwy já hǎa khón lîang
    dék thii hûu pháa-sǎa
    ... dâi yuu sǎi

ຂ້ອຍຈະຫາຄົນລ້ຽງ
ເດັກທີ່ຮູ້ພາສາ
... ໄດ້ຢູ່ໃສ

Can you put an extra bed/cot in the room?
    suay sǒem tịang nái hàwng
    hài dae dâi baw

ຊ່ວຍເສີມຕຽງ
ໃນຫ້ອງໃຫ້ແດ່ໄດ້ບໍ່

I need a car with a child seat.
    khàwy tâwng-kạan lot thii míi
    bawn nâng sǎm-láp dék nâwy

ຂ້ອຍຕ້ອງການລົດທີ່ມີ
ບ່ອນນັ່ງສຳລັບເດັກນ້ອຍ

Is it suitable for children?
    mán máw-sǒm sǎm-láp
    dèk nâwy baw

ມັນເໝາະສົມສຳລັບ
ເດັກນ້ອຍບໍ່

Is there a family discount?
    míi suan lut láa-kháa
    sǎm-láp khâwp khúa baw

ມີສ່ວນລຸດລາຄາ
ສຳລັບຄອບຄົວບໍ່

Do you have a children's menu?
    míi láai-kạan ạa-hǎan
    dék nâwy baw

ມີລາຍການອາຫານ
ເດັກນ້ອຍບໍ່

Are there any activities for children?
    míi kít-já-kạm sǎm-láp
    dék nâwy baw

ມີກິດຈະກຳສຳລັບ
ເດັກນ້ອຍບໍ່

LOOKING FOR A JOB

ການຊອກຫາງານທຳ

Where can I find local
job advertisements?

    khàwy já sâwk hǎa pá-kàat hap
    sá-mak ngáan khó-sá-náa
    dâi yuu sǎi

ຂ້ອຍຈະຊອກຫາ
ປະກາດຮັບສະມັກງານ
ໂຄສະນາໄດ້ຢູ່ໃສ

Do I need a work permit?

    khàwy tâwng-kaan míi bai
    á-nu-nyâat het wîak baw

ຂ້ອຍຕ້ອງການມີໃບ
ອະນຸຍາດເຮັດວຽກບໍ່

I've had experience.

    khàwy míi pá-sóp-kaan

ຂ້ອຍມີປະສົບການ

I've come about the position
advertised.

    khàwy máa pheua tạm-naeng
    thii dâi khó-sá-náa

ຂ້ອຍມາເພື່ອຕຳແໜ່ງ
ທີ່ໄດ້ໂຄສະນາ

I'm ringing about the position
advertised.

    khàwy thóh máa kiaw-káp
    tạm-naeng thii dâi khó-sá-náa

ຂ້ອຍໂທມາກ່ຽວກັບ
ຕຳແໜ່ງທີ່ໄດ້ໂຄສະນາ

What's the wage?

    ngóen dẹuan thao dại

ເງິນເດືອນເທົ່າໃດ

Do I have to pay tax?

    khàwy tâwng sǐa pháa-sǐi baw

ຂ້ອຍຕ້ອງເສຍພາສີບໍ່

I can start ...	khàwy sǎa-mâat loem ...	ຂ້ອຍສາມາດ ເລີ່ມ ...
today	mêu nîi	ມື້ນີ້
tomorrow	mêu eun	ມື້ອື່ນ
next week	ạa-thit nàa	ອາທິດໜ້າ

Useful Words ຄຳສັບທີ່ເປັນປະໂຫຍດ

casual	thám-ma-daa	ທຳມະດາ
employee	lûuk jâang	ລູກຈ້າງ
employer	náai jâang	ນາຍຈ້າງ
full-time	tẹm wéh-láa	ເຕັມເວລາ
job	wîak	ວຽກ
occupation/trade	aa-sîip	ອາຊີບ
part-time	khoeng wéh-láa	ເຄິ່ງເວລາ
resume/cv	síi-wa pá-wat yàw	ຊີວະປະຫວັດຫຍໍ້
traineeship	théun kaan féuk óp-hóm	ທຶນການຝຶກອົບຮົມ
work experience	pá-sóp-kaan het wîak	ປະສົບການເຮັດວຽກ

ON BUSINESS ດຳເນີນທຸລະກິດ

We're attending a ...	phûak háo khào huam ...	ພວກເຈົ້າ ເຂົ້າຮ່ວມ ...
conference	kawng pá-súm	ກອງປະຊຸມ
	săm-ma-náa	ສຳມະນາ
meeting	pá-súm	ປະຊຸມ
trade fair	ngáan wáang	ງານວາງ
	sá-daeng sǐn khâa	ສະແດງສິນຄ້າ
workshop/ seminar	săm-ma-náa	ສຳມະນາ

I'm on a course.
   khàwy kam-láng hían   ຂ້ອຍກຳລັງຮຽນ
I have an appointment with ...
   khàwy míi nat káp ...   ຂ້ອຍມີນັດກັບ ...
Here's my business card.
   nîi maen bát thu-la-kít   ນີ້ແມ່ນບັດທຸລະກິດ
   khǎwng khàwy   ຂອງຂ້ອຍ
I need an interpreter.
   khàwy tâwng-kaan phùu   ຂ້ອຍຕ້ອງການຜູ້
   pae pháa-sǎa   ແປພາສາ

I'd like to use a computer.

khàwy yàak sâi kháwm-pji-tǫe   ຂ້ອຍຢາກໃຊ້ຄອມປິເຕີ

I'd like to send [a fax; an email].

khàwy yàak song fáek/ji-máew   ຂ້ອຍຢາກສົ່ງແຟກ/ອິແມວ

Useful Words   ຄຳສັບທີ່ເປັນປະໂຫຍດ

mobile phone	thóh-la-sáp méu thěu	ໂທລະສັບມືຖື
client	lûuk khàa	ລູກຄ້າ
colleague	pheuan huam ngáan	ເພື່ອນຮ່ວມງານ
distributor	phùu jạm-naai	ຜູ້ຈັດຈຳ່າຍ
email	ji-máew	ອິແມວ
exhibition	ngáan wáang sá-dạeng	ງານວາງສະແດງ
manager	phùu ját kạan	ຜູ້ຈັດການ
profit	kạm-lái	ກຳໄລ
proposal	khàw sá-nǒe	ຂໍ້ສະເໜີ

ON TOUR   ມາທ່ອງທ່ຽວ

We're part of a group.

phûak háo maen ká-lup   ພວກເຮົາແມ່ນກະລຸບ

We're on tour.

phûak háo het thúa   ພວກເຮົາເຣັດທົວ

I'm with the ...	máa káp ...	ມາກັບ ...
group	ká-lup	ກະລຸບ
band	wóng dọn-tjî	ວົງດົນຕີ
team	kha-na phùu lìn	ຄະນະຜູ້ຫລິ້ນ
crew	phûak lûuk méu	ພວກລູກມື

Please speak with our manager.

ká-lu-náa lóm káp phùu   ກະລຸນາລົມກັບຜູ້ຈັດການ
ját kạan phûak háo   ພວກເຮົາ

We've lost our equipment.

phûak háo het kheuang   ພວກເຮົາເຣັດເຄື່ອງ
ú-pá-kạwn sǐa   ອຸປະກອນເສຍ

We sent	phûak háo song	ພວກເຮົາສົ່ງ
equipment	kheuang ú-pá-kawn	ເຄື່ອງອຸປະກອນ
on this ...	tháang ...	ທາງ ...
flight	thìaw bin	ຖ້ຽວບິນ
bus	lot méh	ລົດເມ

We're taking a break of ... days.

phûak háo phak kaan ... mêu ພວກເຮົາພັກການ ... ມື້

We're playing on ...

phûak háo já lìn ... ພວກເຮົາຈະຫລິ້ນ ...

FILM & TV CREWS ຄະນະຖ່າຍທຳແລະ ຄະນະຖ່າຍທຳໂທລະພາບ

We're on location.

phûak háo yuu thii ພວກເຮົາຢູ່ທີ່ສະຖານ
sá-thǎan thii thaai thám ທີ່ຖ່າຍທຳ

We're filming!

kaam-láng thaai thám ກຳລັງຖ່າຍທຳ

May we film here?

thaai thám yuu nîi dâi baw ຖ່າຍທຳຢູ່ນີ້ໄດ້ບໍ່

We're making a ...	phûak háo thaai ...	ພວກເຮົາຖ່າຍ ...
documentary	fím èhk-á-sǎan	ຟິມເອກະສານ
film	nǎng leuang	ໜັງເລື່ອງ
TV series	tawn thóh-la-thát	ຕອນໂທລະທັດ

SPECIFIC NEEDS

PILGRIMAGE & RELIGION

ການເຖິງລິບບູຊາແລະສາສະນາ

I'm ...	khàwy thěu ...	ຂ້ອຍຖື ...
Buddhist	sàat-sá-náa phut	ສາສະນາພຸດ
Christian	sàat-sá-náa khlit	ສາສະນາຄລິດ
Hindu	sàat-sá-náa hín-dụu	ສາສະນາຮິນດູ
Jewish	sàat-sá-náa yíu	ສາສະນາຢິວ
Muslim	sàat-sá-náa mu-sá-lím	ສາສະນາມຸສລິມ

I'm not religious.
   khàwy baw thěu sàat-sá-náa

ຂ້ອຍບໍ່ຖືສາສະນາ

I'm (Catholic), but not practising.
   khàwy maen (kạa-tọh-lik)
   tae baw dâi thěu

ຂ້ອຍແມ່ນ (ກາໂຕລິກ)
ແຕ່ບໍ່ໄດ້ນັບຖື

I think I believe in God.
   khit waa seua thěu
   pha-phùu pẹn jâo

ຄິດວ່າເຊື່ອຖືພະຜູ້ເປັນເຈົ້າ

I believe in destiny.
   khàwy seua thěu sá-tạa-kạm

ຂ້ອຍເຊື່ອຖືສະຕາກັມ

I'm interested in astrology/
philosophy.
   khàwy sǒn jại
   hǒ-la-sàat/pát-sá-yáa

ຂ້ອຍສົນໃຈໂຫລະສາດ/
ປັດສະຍາ

I'm an atheist.
   khàwy baw seua thěu
   pha-phùu pẹn jâo

ຂ້ອຍບໍ່ເຊື່ອຖືພະຜູ້
ເປັນເຈົ້າ

I'm agnostic.
   khàwy seua thěu thám-ma-dàa

ຂ້ອຍເຊື່ອຖືທຳມະດາ

Can I attend this ceremony?
   khàwy sǎa-mâat khào huam
   phi-thíi nîi dâi baw

ຂ້ອຍສາມາດເຂົ້າຮ່ວມ
ພິທີນີ້ໄດ້ບໍ່

Can I pray here?
    sùut món yuu nîi dâi baw   ສູດມົນຢູ່ນີ້ໄດ້ບໍ່
Where can I pray?
    khàwy sǎa-mâat sùut món   ຂ້ອຍສາມາດສູດມົນ
    dâi yuu sǎi   ໄດ້ຢູ່ໃສ

Buddhist temple; monastery	wat	ວັດ
church	bòht khlit	ໂບດຄລິດ
funeral	ngáan	ງານ
	sáa-pạa-na-kít sóp	ຊາປາບະກິດຊົບ
god	pha jâo	ພະເຈົ້າ
monk	khuu-bạa, nak bùat	ຄູບາ ນັກບວດ
prayer	kạan sùut món	ການສູດມົນ
priest	khún phaw	ຄຸນພໍ່
	(nái sàat-sá-náa khlit)	(ໃນສາສະນາຄລິດ)
religious ceremony	phi-thíi kạm sàat-sá-náa	ພິທິກຳສາສະນາ
sabbath	wán sǐn	ວັນສິນ
saint	khón jại pha	ຄົນໃຈພະ
shrine	hǎw wài	ຫໍໄຫວ້
stupa	thâat	ທາດ

A LITTLE IN US ALL ...

The traditional religion of Laos is animism – the belief
that a soul or spirit can be found in all objects, animate or
inanimate. Practice of these beliefs can still be seen today
at Wat Si Muang in Vientiene. Here, the central image of
the temple is the city pillar, where the city's guardian spirit
is said to reside.

SPECIFIC NEEDS

TRACING ROOTS & HISTORY

ຊອກຄົ້ນຫາ ບັນພະບຸລຸດ
ແລະ ປະຫວັດສາດ

I think my ancestors came from this area.

khit waa bạn-pha-bụu-lút
khǎwng khàwy máa jàak
bạw-li-wéhn nîi

ຄິດວ່າບັນພະບຸລຸດຂອງ
ຂ້ອຍມາຈາກ
ບໍລິເວນນີ້

I'm looking for my relatives.

khàwy sâwk hǎa phii-nâwng
khǎwng khàwy

ຂ້ອຍຊອກຫາພີ່ນ້ອງ
ຂອງຂ້ອຍ

I have a relative who lives around here.

khàwy míi phii-nâwng
yuu thii nîi

ຂ້ອຍມີພີ່ນ້ອງ
ຢູ່ທີ່ນີ້

Is there anyone here by the name of ...?

yuu nîi míi khón seu ...

ຢູ່ນີ້ມີຄົນຊື່ ...

I'd like to go to the burial ground.

khàwy yàak pại bawn fǎng sóp

ຂ້ອຍຢາກໄປບ່ອນຝັງສົບ

My (father) was stationed here during the Indochina War.

nái pạang sǒng-kháam
ịn-dụu-jịin phaw khǎwng
khàwy dâi pá-jạm yuu thii nîi

ໃນປາງສົງຄາມອິນດູຈີນ
ພໍ່ຂອງຂ້ອຍໄດ້
ປະຈຳຢູ່ທີ່ນີ້

TIME   ເວລາ

The Lao tell time using a 12-hour system that divides the day into four sections (ຕອນ, tawn). The 'dead of night' period (11 pm to 6 am) is known as kạang khéun (ກາງຄືນ).

6 am to noon	tawn sáo	ຕອນເຊົ້າ
noon to 3 or 4 pm	tawn baai	ຕອນບ່າຍ
3 or 4 pm to 6 pm	tawn láeng	ຕອນແລງ
6 to 11 pm	tawn khám	ຕອນຄ່ຳ

Clock time is expressed in móhng (ໂມງ, hour) and náa-thíi (ນາທີ, minutes), plus one of the above times of day. When speaking, baai (ບ່າຍ, afternoon) comes before the hour; all the other times of day come after.

What time is it?	wéh-láa ják móhng	ເວລາຈັກໂມງ
9 am	kâo móhng sáo	ເກົ້າໂມງເຊົ້າ
midday	thiang	ທ່ຽງ
1 pm	baai móhng	ບ່າຍໂມງ
2.15 pm	baai sǎwng móhng síp-hàa	ບ່າຍສອງໂມງ ສິບຫ້າ
5 pm	hàa móhng láeng	ຫ້າໂມງແລງ
8.20 pm	pàet móhng sáo tawn khám	ແປດໂມງຊາວ ຕອນຄ່ຳ
midnight	thiang khéun	ທ່ຽງຄືນ

When expressing time in terms of number of hours, use sua-móhng (ຊົ່ວໂມງ) rather than móhng.

three hours	sǎam sua-móhng	ສາມຊົ່ວໂມງ

TIME, DATES
& FESTIVALS

DAYS OF THE WEEK   ວັນໃນສັບປະດາ

Sunday	wán ąa-thit	ວັນອາທິດ
Monday	wán jąn	ວັນຈັນ
Tuesday	wán ąng-kháan	ວັນອັງຄານ
Wednesday	wán phut	ວັນພຸດ
Thursday	wán pha-hát	ວັນພະຫັດ
Friday	wán súk	ວັນສຸກ
Saturday	wán săo	ວັນເສົາ

week	ąa-thit	ອາທິດ
weekend	săo-ąa-thit	ເສົາອາທິດ

MONTHS   ເດືອນ

January	dęuan máng-kąwn	ເດືອນມັງກອນ
February	dęuan kųm-pháa	ເດືອນກຸມພາ
March	dęuan mi-náa	ເດືອນມີນາ
April	dęuan méh-săa	ເດືອນເມສາ
May	dęuan pheut-sá-pháa	ເດືອນພຶດສະພາ
June	dęuan mi-thú-náa	ເດືອນມິຖຸນາ
July	dęuan kąw-la-kót	ເດືອນກໍລະກົດ
August	dęuan sĭng-hăa	ເດືອນສິງຫາ
September	dęuan kąn-yáa	ເດືອນກັນຍາ
October	dęuan tú-láa	ເດືອນຕຸລາ
November	dęuan pha-jík	ເດືອນພະຈິກ
December	dęuan than-wáa	ເດືອນທັນວາ

month	dęuan	ເດືອນ
half a month	khoeng dęuan	ເຄິ່ງເດືອນ
a month and a half	dęuan khoeng	ເດືອນເຄິ່ງ

TIME, DATES & FESTIVALS

SEASONS ລະດູ

hot season; dry season (Mar-May)
la-dµu hâwn; la-dµu lâeng ລະດູຮ້ອນ/ລະດູແລ້ງ
rainy season (Jun-Oct)
la-dµu fǒn ລະດູຝົນ
cool season (Nov-Feb)
la-dµu nǎo ລະດູຫນາວ

DATES ວັນທ

The traditional Lao calendar, like the calendars of China, Vietnam, Cambodia and Thailand, is a solar-lunar mix. The year itself is reckoned by solar phases, while the months are divided according to lunar phases (unlike the Gregorian calendar in which months as well as years are reckoned by the sun). The Lao Buddhist Era (BE) calendar figures year one as 543 BC, which means that you must subtract 543 from the Lao calendar year to arrive at the 'Christian era' (Gregorian) calendar familiar in the West (eg, AD 2001 is 2544 BE according to the Lao Buddhist calendar).

Most educated Lao are also familiar with the 'Christian era' (khit sák-á-lâat) calendar.

2544 (BE)
(pháw sǎw) sǎwng phán hàa ສອງພັນຫ້າຮ້ອຍສີ່ສິບສີ່
hâwy sii-síp sii
2001 (AD)
(kháw sǎw) sǎwng phán neung ສອງພັນຫນຶ່ງ

Days of the month are numbered according to the familiar Gregorian calendar.

13th January
wán thíi síp-sǎam dµuan ວັນທີສິບສາມເດືອນ
máng-kạwn ມັງກອນ

date wán thíi ວັນທີ
year pµi ປີ
What date? wán thíi thao-dại? ວັນທີເທົ່າໃດ

TIME, DATES & FESTIVALS

PRESENT ปะจຸບັน

today	mêu nîi	ມື້ນີ້
this evening	láeng nîi	ແລງນີ້
tonight	khéun nîi	ຄືນນີ້
this morning	sâo nîi	ເຊົ້ານີ້
this afternoon	baai nîi	ບ່າຍນີ້
this month	dẹuan nîi	ເດືອນນີ້
all day long	ta-làwt mêu	ຕະຫຼອດມື້

PAST ອາດີດ

yesterday	mêu wáan nîi	ມື້ວານນີ້
the day before yesterday	mêu séun	ມື້ຊືນ
last week	ạa-thit lâew	ອາທິດແລ້ວ
two weeks ago	sǎwng ạa-thit lâew	ສອງອາທິດແລ້ວ
three months ago	sǎam dẹuan lâew	ສາມເດືອນແລ້ວ
four years ago	kawn nîi sii pị̣i	ກ່ອນນີ້ສີ່ປີ

FUTURE ອະນາຄົດ

tomorrow	mêu eun	ມື້ອື່ນ
the day after tomorrow	mêu héu	ມື້ຮື
next week	ạa-thit nàa	ອາທິດໜ້າ
next month	dẹuan nàa	ເດືອນໜ້າ
two more months	ìik sǎwng dẹuan	ອີກສອງເດືອນ

TENSE TONES

You don't need to worry about speaking in the right tense to speak Lao grammatically, but if you want to be understood, remember that Lao is a tonal language – so always be aware that you have to avoid English intonation, such as raising your voice at the end of a question (see page 17 for more help with this).

FESTIVALS & NATIONAL HOLIDAYS

ເທດສະການ
ທາງການແລະວັນພັກ

Festivals in Laos are mostly linked to agricultural seasons or historical Buddhist holidays. The general word for festival in Lao is bųn (ບຸນ, often written as *boun*). Exact dates for festivals may vary from year to year, either because of the lunar calendar – which isn't quite in sync with the Gregorian solar calendar – or because local authorities decide to change festival dates.

On dates noted as public holidays, all government offices and banks will be closed.

February
Magha Puja   ma-khà bųu-sáa   ມະຂະບູຊາ

This day is celebrated on the full moon of the third lunar month to commemorate the preaching of the Buddha to 1250 enlightened monks who came to hear him 'without prior summons'. A public holiday throughout the country, it culminates in a candle-lit walk around the main chapel at every wat.

Late January to early March
Chinese New Year;   kút jíin   ກຸດຈີນ
Vietnamese Tet

Chinese and Vietnamese populations all over Laos celebrate their lunar new year (the date shifts from year to year) with a week of house-cleaning, lion dances and fireworks. The most impressive festivities take place in Vientiane, Pakse and Savannakhet, with parties, deafening nonstop fireworks and visits to Vietnamese and Chinese temples. Chinese- and Vietnamese-run businesses usually close for three days.

April

Lao New Year   pii mai láo   ປີໃໝ່ລາວ

The lunar new year begins in mid-April and practically the entire country comes to a halt and celebrates. Houses are cleaned, people put on new clothes and Buddha images are washed with lustral water. In the wats, offerings of fruit and flowers are made at various altars and votive mounds of sand or stone are fashioned in the courtyards. Later the citizens take to the streets and dowse one another with water, which is an appropriate activity as April is usually the hottest month of the year. This festival is particularly picturesque in Luang Prabang, where it includes elephant processions. The 15th, 16th and 17th of April are official public holidays.

May (Full Moon)

Visakha Puja   wi-săa-khá byu-sáa   ວິສາຄະບູຊາ

This public holiday falls on the 15th day of the waxing moon in the sixth lunar month. It is considered the date of the Buddha's birth, enlightenment and parinibbana, or passing away. Activities are centred around the wat, with candle-lit processions, much chanting and sermonising.

Rocket Festival   bun bâng fái   ບຸນບັ້ງໄຟ

This is a pre-Buddhist rain ceremony that is now celebrated alongside Visakha Puja in Laos and north-east Thailand. This can be one of the wildest festivals in the country, with plenty of music and dance (especially the irreverent măw lám (ໝໍ່ລຳ) performances) processions and general merrymaking, culminating in the firing of bamboo rockets into the sky. In some places, male participants blacken their bodies with lamp soot, while women wear sunglasses and carry carved wooden phalli to imitate men. The firing of the rockets is supposed to prompt the heavens to initiate the rainy season and bring much-needed water to the rice fields.

July

Asanha Puja qa-săn-há bµu-sáa ອາສັນຫະບູຊາ

This public holiday commemorates the first sermon preached by the Buddha.

Mid to late July (Full Moon)

Rains Retreat khào phán-săa ເຂົ້າພັນສາ
Opening (khào wat-săa) (ເຂົ້າວັດສາ)

This is the beginning of the traditional three-month 'rains retreat', during which Buddhist monks are expected to station themselves in a single monastery. At other times of year they are allowed to travel from wat to wat or simply to wander in the countryside, but during the rainy season they forego the wandering so as not to damage fields of rice or other crops. This is also the traditional time of year for men to enter the monkhood temporarily, hence many ordinations take place.

August/September (Full Moon)

Ancestor Respect haw khào pá-dáp dịn ຫໍເຂົ້າປະດັບດິນ

This is a sombre festival in which the living pay respect to the dead. Many cremations take place during this time and gifts are presented to the Sangha (Buddhist clergy) so that monks will chant on behalf of the deceased. Families visit bone stupas (ທາດກະດູກ, thàat ká-dùuk) with offerings of candles, incense and flowers.

TIME, DATES & FESTIVALS

October/November (Full Moon)

Rains Retreat   àwk phán-săa   ออกพันสา
Closing   (àwk wat-săa)   (ออกวัดสา)

This celebrates the end of the 3-month Rains Retreat. Monks are allowed to leave the monasteries to travel and are presented with robes, alms-bowls and other requisites of the renunciative life. A second festival held in association with Awk Phansaa is the Bụn Nâam (Water Festival). Boat races are commonly held in towns located on rivers, such as Vientiane, Luang Prabang and Savannakhet.

Pha That Luang   bụn pha thâat lŭang   บุນພะທາດຫລວງ
Festival

This takes place at Pha That Luang in Vientiane. Hundreds of monks assemble to receive alms and floral votives early in the morning on the first day of the festival, and there's a colourful procession between Pha That Luang and Wat Si Muang. The celebration lasts a week and includes fireworks and music, culminating in a candlelit circumambulation of That Luang.

December

Lao National Day   wán sâat láo   อันຊาດລาວ

The 2nd of December marks the 1975 victory of the proletariat over the monarchy with parades and speeches. It is a public holiday.

December/January

Prince Vessantara   bụn pha wêht   ບຸນພະເວດ
Festival

This is a temple-centred festival in which the *jataka* or birth-tale of Prince Vessantara, the Buddha's penultimate life, is recited. This is also a favoured time (second to khào phán-sǎa) for Lao males to be ordained into the monkhood. The scheduling of Bun Pha Wet is staggered so that it is held on different days in different villages. This is so that relatives and friends living in different villages can invite one another to their respective celebrations.

New Year's Day   wán pịi mai sǎa-kọn   ວັນປີໃໝ່ສາກົນ

A recent public holiday in deference to the Western calendar.

Useful Words & Phrases

ບາງຄຳສັບແລະປະໂຫຍກທີ່
ເປັນປະໂຫຍດ

always	lêuay lêuay	ເລື້ອຍໆ
annual	thuk pįi	ທຸກປີ
before	kawn	ກອນ
century	sá-tá-wat	ສະຕະວັດ
closed	pít	ປິດ
dawn	tąa-wán khèun	ຕາວັນຂຶ້ນ
daytime	kąang wán	ກາງວັນ
early	sâo	ເຊົ້າ
evening	láeng	ແລງ
every day	thuk wán	ທຸກວັນ
forever	tá-làwt kąan	ຕະຫລອດການ
holiday	wán phak kąan	ວັນພັກການ
late	sâa	ຊ້າ
night	khám	ຄ່ຳ
now	diaw nîi; tąwn nîi	ດຽວນີ້/ຕອນນີ້
nowadays	sá-mǎi nîi	ສະໄໝນີ້
open	pòet	ເປີດ
period (era)	sá-mǎi	ສະໄໝ
period (interval)	wéh-láa	ເວລາ
sometimes	bąang theua	ບາງເທື່ອ
time	wéh-láa	ເວລາ
on time	kǫng taw wéh-láa	ກົງຕໍ່ເວລາ
in time	seu wéh-láa	ຊື່ເວລາ
until	jǫn kwaa	ຈົນກ່ວາ
when (conjunction)	mêua/wéh-láa	ເມື່ອ/ເວລາ
when (what date?)	mêua-dąi	ເມື່ອໃດ
whenever	mêua-dąi kaw-tąam	ເມື່ອໃດກໍ່ຕາມ

ນຳເບີ້ແລະຈຳນວນ

See the Grammar section for important information on how to use 'classifiers' or 'counters' with Lao numbers.

CARDINAL NUMBERS ເລກນັບ

zero	sŭun	ສູນ
one	neung	ໜຶ່ງ
two	sǎwng	ສອງ
three	sǎam	ສາມ
four	sii	ສີ່
five	hàa	ຫ້າ
six	hók	ຫົກ
seven	jét	ເຈັດ
eight	pàet	ແປດ
nine	kâo	ເກົ້າ
10	síp	ສິບ
11	síp-ét	ສິບເອັດ
12	síp-sǎwng	ສິບສອງ
13	síp-sǎam	ສິບສາມ
14	síp-sii	ສິບສີ່
...-teen	síp-...	ສິບ ...
20	sáo	ຊາວ
21	sáo-ét	ຊາວເອັດ
22	sáo-sǎwng	ຊາວສອງ
23	sáo-sǎam	ຊາວສາມ
30	sǎam-síp	ສາມສິບ
40	sii-síp	ສີ່ສິບ
50	hàa-síp	ຫ້າສິບ
60	hók-síp	ຫົກສິບ
70	jét-síp	ເຈັດສິບ
80	pàet-síp	ແປດສິບ
90	kâo-síp	ເກົ້າສິບ

100	hâwy	ຮ້ອຍ
200	sǎwng hâwy	ສອງຮ້ອຍ
300	sǎam hâwy	ສາມຮ້ອຍ
1000	phán	ພັນ
10,000	meun (síp-phán)	ໝື່ນ (ສິບພັນ)
100,000	sǎen (hâwy phán)	ແສນ (ຮ້ອຍພັນ)
million	lâan	ລ້ານ
billion	têu (phan láan)	ຕື້

ORDINAL NUMBERS   ເລກລຳດັບ

These are formed by adding thíi (ທີ່) before the cardinal numbers.

first	thíi neung	ທີ່ໜຶ່ງ
second	thíi sǎwng	ທີ່ສອງ
thirty-first	thíi sǎam-síp-ét	ທີ່ສາມສິບເອັດ

FRACTIONS   ເລກສ່ວນ

Fractions are formed by inserting suan (ສ່ວນ, part) before the lower integer. 'Half' has its own term, khoeng (ເຄິ່ງ).

one quarter (1/4)	neung suan sìi	ໜຶ່ງສ່ວນສີ່
one eighth (1/8)	neung suan pàet	ໜຶ່ງສ່ວນແປດ
three eighths (3/8)	sǎam suan pàet	ສາມສ່ວນແປດ
half (1/2)	khoeng	ເຄິ່ງ

NUMBERS & AMOUNTS

Useful Words   ບາງຄຳສັບທີ່ເປັນປະໂຫຍດ

count	nap	ນັບ
couple/pair	khuu	ຄູ່
decimal point	jút	ຈຸດ
dozen	lǒh	ໂຫຼ
equal (adj)	thao kạn	ເທົ່າກັນ
equal to	thao káp	ເທົ່າກັບ
large	nyai	ໃຫຍ່
least	nâwy thii-sút	ນ້ອຍທີ່ສຸດ
little/few	nâwy	ນ້ອຍ
many	lǎai	ຫຼາຍ

NUMBERS & AMOUNTS

minus	lop	ລົບ
most	lǎai thii-sút	ຫລາຍທີ່ສຸດ
much	lǎai	ຫລາຍ
number (amount)	jạm-núan	ຈຳນວນ
number (numeral)	nâm-bǫe (lêhk)	ນ້ຳເບີ້(ເລກ)
plus	pá-sǒm/buak	ປະສົມ/ບວກ
small	nâwy	ນ້ອຍ
weight	nâm-nak	ນ້ຳໜັກ

Help!	suay dae	ຊ່ວຍແດ່
It's an emergency!	súk sŏen	ສຸກເສີນ
Stop!	yút	ຢຸດ
Go away!	nĭi pại	ໜີໄປ
Watch out!	la-wáng	ລະວັງ
Thief!	khá-móhy (jọhn)	ຂະໂມຍ (ໂຈນ)
Fire!	fái mài	ໄຟໄໝ້

There's been an accident!
  míi ú-bát-tí-het

Call a doctor!
  suay ôen thaan mǎw
  hài dae

Call an ambulance!
  suay ôen lot hóhng
  mǎw dae

Call the police!
  suay ôen tam-lùat dae

I've been robbed.
  khàwy thèuk khá-móhy

I've been raped.
  khàwy thèuk khòm khěun

I'll get the police.
  khàwy sii ôen tam-lùat

ມີອຸບັດຕິເຫດ

ຊ່ວຍເອີ້ນທ່ານໝໍ
ໃຫ້ແດ່

ຊ່ວຍເອີ້ນລົດໂຮງ
ໝໍແດ່

ຊ່ວຍເອີ້ນຕຳຫລວດແດ່

ຂ້ອຍຖືກຂະໂມຍ

ຂ້ອຍຖືກຂົ່ມຂືນ

ຂ້ອຍຊິເອີ້ນຕຳຫລວດ

EMERGENCIES

Useful Phrases ปะໂຫຍກທີ່ເປັນປະໂຫຍດ

Could you help me please?
jâo suay khàwy dâi baw
เจົ້າຊ່ວຍຂ້ອຍໄດ້ບໍ່

I am ill.
khàwy puay
ຂ້ອຍປ່ວຍ

I have health insurance.
khàwy míi pá-kạn phái
sú-khá-phâap
ຂ້ອຍມີປະກັນໄພ
ສຸຂະພາບ

My blood group is (A, B, O, AB)
positive/negative.
lêuat khàwy maen klúp
(A, B, O, AB) bùak/lop
เลือดຂ້ອຍແມ່ນກລຸບ
(A, B, O, AB) ບວກ/ລົບ

I am lost.
khàwy lǒng tháang
ຂ້ອຍຫລົງທາງ

Where are the toilets?
hàwng nâm yuu sǎi
ຫ້ອງນ້ຳຢູ່ໃສ

Could I please use the telephone?
sâi thóh-la-sáp dâi baw
ໃຊ້ໂທລະສັບໄດ້ບໍ່

POLICE ຕຳຫລວດ

Where's the police station?
sa-thǎa-níi tam-lùat yuu sǎi
ສະຖານີຕຳຫລວດຢູ່ໃສ

My ... was/were stolen.	... khǎwng khàwy thèuk khá-móhy	... ຂອງຂ້ອຍຖືກ ຂະໂມຍ
I've lost my ...	khàwy het ... sǐa lâew	ຂ້ອຍເຮັດ ... ເສຍແລ້ວ
bags	kọng kheuang	ຖົງເຄື່ອງ
money	ngóen	ເງິນ
travellers cheques	saek dọen tháang	ແຊັກເດີນທາງ
passport	nǎng-sěu phaan dạen	ໜັງສືຜ່ານ ແດນ

I would like to contact my
embassy/consulate.

    yàak tít taw sa-thǎan-thûut   ຢາກຕິດຕໍ່ສະຖານທູດ
    khǎwng khàwy   ຂອງຂ້ອຍ

I speak (English).

    khàwy wâo pháa-sǎa (ạng-kít)   ຂ້ອຍເວົ້າພາສາ (ອັງກິດ)

I understand.

    khàwy khào jại   ຂ້ອຍເຂົ້າໃຈ

I don't understand.

    khàwy baw khào jại   ຂ້ອຍບໍ່ເຂົ້າໃຈ

I didn't realise I was doing
anything wrong.

    khàwy baw húu dâi het   ຂ້ອຍບໍ່ຮູ້ໄດ້ເຮັດ
    nyǎng phít   ຫຍັງຜິດ

I didn't do it.

    khàwy baw dâi het   ຂ້ອຍບໍ່ໄດ້ເຮັດ

I'm sorry, I apologise.

    khǎw thôht, sǐa jại   ຂໍໂທດເສຍໃຈ

My contact number in case of
emergency (next of kin) is ...

    khàwp khúa thii já hài tít taw   ຄອບຄົວທີ່ຈະໃຫ້ຕິດຕໍ່ໃນ
    nái káw-la-níi súk sǒen ...   ກໍລະນີສຸກເສີນ ...

EMERGENCIES

A

to be able (can)	dâi	ໄດ້
I can. khàwy dâi		ຂ້ອຍໄດ້
I can't. khàwy baw dâi		ຂ້ອຍບໍ່ໄດ້
Can you ...? jâo dâi baw ...		ເຈົ້າໄດ້ບໍ່ ...
about (approximately)	pá-máan	ປະມານ
above (adv)	tháang thóeng	ທາງເທິງ
above (prep)	yuu thóeng	ຢູ່ເທິງ
abroad	taang pá-thêht	ຕ່າງປະເທດ
to accept	hap	ຮັບ
I accept. khàwy hap		ຂ້ອຍຮັບ
Do you accept? jâo hap baw		ເຈົ້າຮັບບໍ່
accident	ú-bát-tí-hèht	ອຸບັຕິເຫດ
accommodation	bawn phak	ບ່ອນພັກ
addiction	sèhp tít	ເສບຕິດ
address	thii yuu	ທີ່ຢູ່
administration	kǫan ját tãng	ການຈັດຕັ້ງ
admission (entry)	phaan khào	ຜ່ານເຂົ້າ
admission fee	khaa phaan pá-tǫu	ຄ່າຜ່ານປະຕູ
to admit (allow entry)	á-nu-nyâat khào	ອະນຸຍາດເຂົ້າ
adult	phùu nyai	ຜູ້ໃຫຍ່
adventure	pá-jǫn phái	ປະຈິນໄພ
aeroplane	héua bin	ເຮືອບິນ
by aeroplane	dǫhy héua bin	ໂດຍເຮືອບິນ
after	lãng jàak	ຫຼັງຈາກ

again	ìik	ອີກ
against	tâan	ຕ້ານ
to agree	hĕn dǐi	ເຫັນດີ

I agree. khàwy hĕn dǐi	ຂ້ອຍເຫັນດີ
Do you agree? jâo hĕn dǐi baw	ເຈົ້າເຫັນດີບໍ່
Agreed! tók-lóng	ຕົກລົງ

agriculture	ká-sí-kạm	ກະສິກຳ
ahead	kawn	ກ່ອນ
aid	suay lĕua	ຊ່ວຍເຫຼືອ
AIDS	lôhk èht	ໂລກເອດສ
airline	sǎi kạan bịn	ສາຍການບິນ
airmail	tháang qa-kàat	ທາງອາກາດ
by airmail	dọhy tháang qa-kàat	ໂດຍທາງອາກາດ
alarm clock	móhng púk	ໂມງປຸກ
all	tháng mót	ທັງໝົດ
allergy	phúum phàe	ພູມແພ້
to allow	á-nu-mat	ອະນຸມັດ
almost	kèuap	ເກືອບ
alone	dòht diaw	ໂດດດ່ຽວ
also	khéu/teum	ຄື/ຕື່ມ
alternative	tháang lêuak	ທາງເລືອກ
always	lêuay lêuay	ເລື້ອຍໆ
amazing	ma-hat-sá-jạn	ມະຫັດສະຈັນ
ambassador	èhk-ák-kha-lat-thá-thûut	ເອກອັກຄະລັດຖະທູດ
ambulance	lot hóng măw	ລົດໂຮງໝໍ
among	la-waang	ລະຫວ່າງ
ancient	bọh-háan	ໂບຮານ
and	lae	ແລະ

B

angry	hâai	ຮ້າຍ
antique (adj)	kheuang bọh-háan	ເຄື່ອງໂບຮານ
any	eun-dại	ອື່ນໃດ
anytime	wéh-láa dại kaw dâi	ເວລາໃດກໍໄດ້
apartment	ạa-kháan	ອາຄານ
appointment	kạan nat phop	ການນັດພົບ
approximately	pá-máan	ປະມານ
archaeological	bụu-háan-na-kha-dịi	ບູຮານມະຕະຄີ
to argue	thók thĩang	ຖົກຖຽງ
argument	kạan thók thĩang	ການຖົກຖຽງ
to arrive	máa hâwt	ມາຮອດ
art	sĭi-la-pá	ສິລະປະ
to ask	thăam	ຖາມ
at (place)	yuu thii	ຢູ່ທີ່
at (time)	nái wéh-láa	ໃນເວລາ
automatic	ọh-tọh-nóh-mat	ໂອໂຕໂນມັດ

B

baby	dék nâwy	ເດັກນ້ອຍ
back	lăng	ຫລັງ
backpack	bạa-lóh; thŏng pêh	ບາໂລ; ຖົງເປ້
bad	sua	ຊົ່ວ
bag	kheuang/thŏng	ເຄື່ອງ/ຖົງ
baggage	ká-pạo kheuang	ກະເປົາເຄື່ອງ
ball (object)	màak bạan	ໝາກບານ
bank	tha-náa-kháan	ທະນາຄານ
bar	bạa	ບາ
to bathe	àap nâm	ອາບນ້ຳ
bathers (swimsuit)	sut láwy nâm	ຊຸດລອຍນ້ຳ
women's	khăwng mae nýing	ຂອງແມ່ຍິງ
men's	khăwng phùu sáai	ຂອງຜູ້ຊາຍ
bathroom	hàwng nâm	ຫ້ອງນ້ຳ

**D
I
C
T
I
O
N
A
R
Y**

battery	thaan fái săi; màw fái	ໝໍໄຟ
beautiful	ngáam	ງາມ
because	phaw-waa	ເພາະວ່າ
bed	tiang	ຕຽງ
before (conj)	kawn	ກ່ອນ
before (prep)	kawn	ກ່ອນ
beggar	khón kháw tháan	ຄົນຂໍທານ
to begin	loem	ເລີ່ມ
beginner	phùu loem tôn	ຜູ້ເລີ່ມຕົ້ນ
behind	tháang lăng	ທາງຫຼັງ
below (adv)	yuu lum	ຢູ່ລຸ່ມ
below (prep)	bêuang lum	ເບື້ອງລຸ່ມ
beside	khàang káp	ຂ້າງກັບ
best	dìi thii-sút	ດີທີ່ສຸດ
better	dìi kwaa	ດີກ່ວາ
between (prep)	la-waang	ລະຫວ່າງ
Bible	tạm-láa sǎa-sa-náa khlit	ຕຳລາສາສະບາຄລິດ
bicycle	lot thìip	ລົດຖີບ
big	nyai	ໃຫຍ່
bill	bại bịin	ໃບບິນ
birthday	wán kòet	ວັນເກີດ
to bite	kát	ກັດ
bitter	khŏm	ຂົມ
blanket	phàa hom	ຜ້າຫົ່ມ
to bless	yay pháwn	ອວຍພອນ
blind	tạa bàwt	ຕາບອດ
blood	lêuat	ເລືອດ
boat	héua	ເຮືອ
bomb	la-bòet	ລະເບີດ

| Bon appetit! | |
| sóen sâep | ເຊີນແຊບ |

| book | pêum | ປຶ້ມ |
| bookshop | hàan khăai pêum | ຮ້ານຂາຍປຶ້ມ |

| bored | beua naai | ເບື່ອໜ່າຍ |

I'm bored.
khàwy beua — ຂ້ອຍເບື່ອ

| border | sáai dạen | ຊາຍແດນ |
| to borrow | yéum | ຍືມ |

May I borrow this?
khăw yéum dae — ຂໍຍືມແດ່

boss	náai	ນາຍ
both	tháng săwng	ທັງສອງ
bottle opener	kheuang khăi kâew	ເຄື່ອງໄຂແກ້ວ
boy	dék sáai	ເດັກຊາຍ
brake(s)	hàam	ຫ້າມ
bread	khào jìi	ເຂົ້າຈີ່
to break	tàek	ແຕກ
breakfast	qa-hăan sáo	ອາຫານເຊົ້າ
to breathe	hăai jai	ຫາຍໃຈ
bribe	sĩn bọn	ສິນບົນ
to bribe	hài sĩn bọn	ໃຫ້ສິນບົນ
bridge	khŭa	ຂົວ
bright	jâeng	ແຈ້ງ
to bring	qo máa	ເອົາມາ

Can you bring it?
jâo qo máa dâi baw — ເຈົ້າເອົາມາໄດ້ບໍ່

broken	phéh lâew	ເພແລ້ວ
bucket	khú sai nâm	ຄຸໃສ່ນ້ຳ
building	qa-kháan	ອາຄານ
to burn	jút/mâi	ຈຸດ/ໄໝ້
bus	lot méh	ລົດເມ
business	thu-la-kít	ທຸລະກິດ
busy	kháa wîak; nyùng	ຄາວຽກ; ຫຍຸ້ງ
but	tae waa	ແຕ່ວ່າ

| to buy | sêu | ຊື້ |

Where did you buy this?
jâo sêu nïi máa tae säi   ເຈົ້າຊື້ ນີ້ມາແຕ່ໃສ

C

cafe	hâan kạa-féh	ຮ້ານກາເຟ
camera	kâwng thaai hûup	ກ້ອງຖ່າຍຮູບ
to camp	tâng khêm	ຕັ້ງເຄັ້ມ
can (tin)	ká-pạwng	ກະປ໋ອງ
can	dâi	ໄດ້

Can I take a photograph?
thaai hûup dâi baw   ຖ່າຍຮູບໄດ້ບໍ່

No, you can't.
baw dâi   ບໍ່ໄດ້

cancel	yok lôek	ຍົກເລີກ
can opener	kheuang khäi ká-pạwng	ເຄື່ອງໄຂກະປ໋ອງ
candle	thían	ທຽນ
capital (city)	na-kháwn lüang	ນະຄອນຫລວງ
capitalism	théun-ni-nyom	ທຶນນິຍົມ
car	lot	ລົດ
cards (playing)	phâi	ໄພ້
to care	dyu-láe	ດູແລ

I don't care.
khàwy baw sön   ຂ້ອຍບໍ່ສົນ

Careful!
la-wáng   ລະວັງ

| to carry | qo máa | ເອົາມາ |

I'll carry it.
khàwy já qo máa   ຂ້ອຍຈະເອົາມາ

| CD | phaen síi-dịi | ແຜ່ນຊີດີ |

C

to celebrate	sá-lăwng	ສະຫລອງ
cemetery	paa sâa	ປ່າຊ້າ
certificate	bại yang-yéun	ໃບຢັ້ງຢືນ
certain (sure)	nae náwn	ແນ່ນອນ

Are you certain?
jâo nae jại baw ເຈົ້າແນ່ໃຈບໍ່

chair	tang nang	ຕັ່ງນັ່ງ
chance	oh-kàat	ໂອກາດ
by chance	dọhy bạng ọen	ໂດຍບັງເອີນ
change (money)	ngóen nâwy	ເງິນນ້ອຍ
cheap	thèuk	ຖືກ
cheese	nóei	ເນີຍ
chemist	phùu khăai yáa	ຜູ້ຂາຍຢາ
child	dék nâwy	ເດັກນ້ອຍ
chocolate	khào-nŏm sóh-koh-laet	ເຂົ້າໜົມໂຊໂກແລັດ
to choose	lêuak	ເລືອກ
church	bòht khlit	ໂບດຄລິດ
cigarettes	yáa sùup	ຢາສູບ
cinema	hóng hùup ngáo	ໂຮງຮູບເງົາ
city	méuang	ເມືອງ
city centre	jại káang méuang	ໃຈກາງເມືອງ
clean (adj)	khwáam sá-àat	ຄວາມສະອາດ
close (nearby)	kâi	ໄກ້
to close	át/pít	ອັດ/ປິດ

It's closed.
pít lâew ປິດແລ້ວ

clothing	kheuang nung	ເຄື່ອງນຸ່ງ
coin	ngóen lĭan	ເງິນຫລຽນ
cold (adj; climate)	năo	ໜາວ
cold (n)	khwáam năo	ຄວາມໜາວ

D
I
C
T
I
O
N
A
R
Y

colour	sĭi	ສີ
to come	máa	ມາ
comfortable	sá-bại	ສະບາຍ
communism	la-bàwp kháwm-múu-nit	ລະບອບຄອມມູນິດ
company (business)	bạw-li-sat	ບໍລິສັດ
complex (adj)	nyùng nyĕuang	ຫຍຸ້ງເຫຍື້ອງ
condom	thŏng yáang á-náa-mái	ຖົງຢາງອະນາໄມ
to confirm	yéun yán	ຍືນຍັນ

Congratulations!
sóm sòei ຊົມເຊີຍ

constipation	nyeung tháwng	ຍັ້ງທ້ອງ
consulate	kọng-sŭun	ກົງສຸນ
contact lens	waen sai kâew tạa	ແວ່ນໃສ່ແກ້ວຕາ
contagious	pha-nyâat tit-taw	ພະຍາດຕິດຕໍ່
contraceptive	sing khúm kạm-nòet	ສິ່ງຄຸມກຳເນີດ
conversation	kạan sŏn-tha-náa	ການສົນທະນາ
to cook	taeng kịn	ແຕ່ງກິນ
corner (of a room)	jae hâwng	ແຈຫ້ອງ
corner (of a street)	tháang nyâek	ທາງແຍກ
at/on the corner	yuu tháang nyâek	ຢູ່ທາງແຍກ
corrupt (adj)	kịn sĭn bọn	ກິນສິນບົນ
corruption	kạan kịn sĭn bọn	ການກິນສິນບົນ
cost	láa-kháa	ລາຄາ
to cost	míi láa-kháa	ມີລາຄາ

It costs ...
mán míi láa-kháa ... ມັນມີລາຄາ ...

How much does it cost?
láa-kháa thao dại ລາຄາເທົ່າໃດ

| to cough | ại | ໄອ |
| to count | nap | ນັບ |

crazy	bâa	ບ້າ
credit card	bát khréh-dit	ບັດເຄຣດິດ
crop	phôn-la-pùuk	ຜົນລະປູກ
cross (angry)	khìat khâen	ຢຸດແໝ້ນ
customs office	hàwng-kaan	ຫ້ອງການພາສີ
	pháa-sǐi ɑa-kɑwn	ອາກອນ
to cut	tát	ຕັດ
to cycle	khìi lot thiip	ຂີ່ລົດຖີບ

D

dad	phaw	ພໍ່
daily	pá-jɑm wán	ປະຈຳວັນ
damp	jêun	ຈຶ້ນ
to dance	fâwn	ຟ້ອນ
dangerous	ɑn-ta-láai	ອັນຕະລາຍ
dark	mêut	ມືດ
date (time)	wán thíi	ວັນທີ
date of birth	wán kòet	ວັນເກີດ
dawn	ɑa-lún	ອາລຸມ
day	kɑang wén	ກາງເວັນ
dead	tɑai lâew	ຕາຍແລ້ວ
deaf	hǔu nùak	ຫູໜວກ
death	khwáam tɑai	ຄວາມຕາຍ
to decide	tát sǐn jɑi	ຕັດສິນໃຈ
decision	kɑan tát sǐn jɑi	ການຕັດສິນໃຈ
delay	jó	ໂຈະ
delicious	sâep	ແຊບ
delightful	muan seun	ມ່ວນຊື່ນ
democracy	pá-sáa-thi-pá-tɑi	ປະຊາທິປະໄຕ
demonstration	kɑan dɑen khá-buan	ການເດິນຂະບວນ
(protest)		

to depart (leave)	àwk	ອອກ

The flight departs at ...
thìaw bịn àwk ...   ຖ້ຽວບິນອອກ ...

What time does it leave?
àwk jàk móhng   ອອກຈັກໂມງ

department store	hàan sap-pha-sĭn-khâa	ຮ້ານຊັບພະສິນຄ້າ
departure	kạan àwk	ການອອກ
to destroy	thám láai	ທຳລາຍ
development	kạan phat-tha-náa	ການພັດທະນາ
diabetes	lôhk bạo-wăan	ໂລກເບົາຫວານ
dictionary	pêum wat-já-náa-nu-kọm	ປຶ້ມວັດຈະນານຸກົມ
different	tàek-taang	ແຕກຕ່າງ
difficult	nyàak	ຫຍາກ

It's difficult.
nyùng nyàak   ຫຍຸ້ງຫຍາກ

dinner	ạa-hăan láeng	ອາຫານແລງ
direct	dọhy kọng	ໂດຍກົງ
direction (adv)	thit tháang	ທິດທາງ
dirt	dịn	ດິນ
dirty	pêuan	ເປື້ອນ
disabled person	khón phi-kạan	ຄົນພິການ
discount	lut láa-kháa	ລຸດລາຄາ
discrimination	kạan jạm-nâek	ການຈຳແນກ
disinfectant	yáa khàa sêua	ຢາຂ້າເຊື້ອ
distant	kại	ໄກ
to do	het	ເຮັດ

I'll do it.
khàwy sĭi het   ຂ້ອຍຊິເຮັດ

Can you do that?
jào het dâi baw   ເຈົ້າເຮັດໄດ້ບໍ່

Don't do it.		
yáa het		ຢ່າເຮັດ
doctor	thaan măw	ທ່ານໝໍ
dog	măa	ໝາ
doll	hun	ຮຸ່ນ
door	pá-tuu	ປະຕູ
double	khuu	ຄູ່
double bed	tiang khuu	ຕຽງຄູ່
double room	hàwng khuu	ຫ້ອງຄູ່
down	lum	ລຸ່ມ
downtown	kạang méuang	ກາງເມືອງ
dream	khwáam făn	ຄວາມຝັນ
to dream	făn	ຝັນ
to dress	nung	ນຸ່ງ
dried	hàeng	ແຫ້ງ
drink	kheuang deum	ເຄື່ອງດື່ມ
to drink	deum	ດື່ມ

I don't drink spirits.		
khàwy baw kịn lào		ຂ້ອຍບໍ່ກິນເຫຼົ້າ
Do you drink beer?		
jảo kịn bịa baw		ເຈົ້າກິນເບຍບໍ່

drinkable	pẹn tạa deum	ເປັນຕາດື່ມ
drinkable water	nâm deum	ນ້ຳດື່ມ
to drive	kháp	ຂັບ (ລົດ)
drivers licence	bại á-nu-nyâat	ໃບອະນຸຍາດຂັບຂີ່
	kháp-khii	
drugs (illegal)	yáa sèhp tít	ຢາເສບຕິດ
drunk (inebriated)	máo lào	ເມົາເຫຼົ້າ
dry (adj)	hàeng	ແຫ້ງ
during	la-waang	ລະຫວ່າງ
dust	khii fun	ຂີ້ຝຸ່ນ

E

each	tae-la	ແຕ່ລະ
early	tae sáo	ແຕ່ເຊົ້າ
to earn	dâi	ໄດ້
earnings	láai hap	ລາຍຮັບ
Earth	nuay lôhk	ໜ່ວຍໂລກ
earthquake	phaen-dịn wǎi	ແຜ່ນດິນໄຫວ
east	thit tọa-wén àwk	ທິດຕາເວັນອອກ
easy	ngaai	ງ່າຍ
to eat	kịn	ກິນ
economical	pá-yat	ປະຍັດ
economics	sèht-thá-sàat	ເສດຖະສາດ
economy	sèht-thá-kit	ເສດຖະກິດ
economy (thrift)	kạan pá-yat	ການປະຍັດ
education	kạan séuk-sǎa	ການສຶກສາ
elections	kạan lêuak tàng	ການເລືອກຕັ້ງ
electricity	fái fâa	ໄຟຟ້າ
elevator (lift)	lip (khân dại fái fâa)	ລິບ (ຂັ້ນໄດໄຟຟ້າ)
email	ịi-máew	ອີແມວ
embassy	sá-thǎan thûut	ສະຖານທູດ
emergency exit	tháang àwk súk sǒen	ທາງອອກສຸກເສີນ
employer	náai jàang	ນາຍຈ້າງ
empty	pao	ເປົ່າ
end	jóp	ຈົບ
energy	pha-láng-ngáan	ພະລັງງານ
English	pháa-sǎa ạng-kít	ພາສາອັງກິດ
to enjoy (oneself)	muan	ມ່ວນ
enough	phaw	ພໍ
to enter	khào	ເຂົ້າ
entrance	tháang khào	ທາງເຂົ້າ
entry	kạan-khào	ການເຂົ້າ

environment	sing wâet-lâwm	ສິ່ງແວດລ້ອມ
equal (adj)	thao káp	ເທົ່າກັບ
European (person)	khón yúu-lôhp	ຄົນຢູໂລບ
evening	tawn khám	ຕອນຄ່ຳ
event	ngáan thêht-sá-kaan	ງານເທດສະການ
every	thuk-thuk/tae-la	ທຸກໆ/ແຕ່ລະ
every day	thuk wán	ທຸກວັນ
everyone	thuk khón	ທຸກຄົນ
everything	thuk yaang	ທຸກຢ່າງ
example	tua yaang	ຕົວຢ່າງ
for example	yok tua yaang	ຍົກຕົວຢ່າງ
to exchange	lâek pian	ແລກປ່ຽນ

Excuse me. khǎw thôht		ຂໍໂທດ

exhausted	meuay	ເໝື່ອຍ
exhibition	wáang sá-daeng	ວາງສະແດງ
exile	phùu theuk néh-la-thêht	ຜູ້ຖືກເນລະເທດ
to exile	néh-la-thêht	ເນລະເທດ
exit	tháang àwk	ທາງອອກ
expensive	pháeng	ແພງ
experience	pá-sóp-kaan	ປະສົບການ
export	sîn-khâa song àwk	ສິນຄ້າສົ່ງອອກ
to export	song àwk sîn-khâa	ສົ່ງອອກສິນຄ້າ
eye	taa	ຕາ

F

false (wrong)	phít	ຜິດ
false (fake)	pawm	ປອມ
family	khâwp khúa	ຄອບຄົວ
fan (cooling)	phat lóm	ພັດລົມ

fan (sports)	khǎa khĭa	ຂາເຊຍ
far	kai	ໄກ
farm	bawn phá-lit ká-sí-kam	ບ່ອນຜະລິດກະສິກຳ
fast (adj)	wái	ໄວ
to fast	ngot kin aa-hǎan	ງົດກິນອາຫານ
fat (adj)	tûi	ຕຸ້ຍ
fat	khǎi mán	ໄຂມັນ
father	phaw	ພໍ່
fault	khwáam phít phâat	ຄວາມຜິດພາດ
It's my fault.		
khwáam phít khǎwng khàwy		ຄວາມຜິດຂອງຂ້ອຍ
fear	khwáam yâan	ຄວາມຢ້ານ
fee	láa-kháa	ລາຄາ
to feel	hûu-séuk	ຮູ້ສຶກ
feeling	khwáam-hûu-séuk	ຄວາມຮູ້ສຶກ
ferry	héua dohy-sǎan	ເຮືອໂດຍສານ
festival	ngáan bun	ງານບຸນ
fever	khài	ໄຂ້
few	nàwy	ໜ້ອຍ
a few	nàwy diaw	ໜ້ອຍດຽວ
fiance(e)	khuu màn	ຄູ່ໝັ້ນ
film (movie)	hûup ngáo	ຮູບເງົາ
film (roll of)	fím thaai hûup	ຟິມຖ່າຍຮູບ
filtered (water)	nâm kawng	ນ້ຳ ກອງ
fine (penalty)	páp mǎi	ປັບໃໝ
fire	fái	ໄຟ
firewood	féun	ຟືນ
first	thii neung	ທີ່ໜຶ່ງ
fish	paa	ປາ
flag	thúng	ທຸງ

flashlight (torch)	fái sǎai	ໄຟສາຍ
flight	thìaw bịn	ຖ້ຽວບິນ
flood	ú-thok-ká-phái	ອຸທົກກະໄພ
floor	phêun	ພື້ນ
on the floor	yuu phêun	ຢູ່ພື້ນ
flower(s)	dàwk mâi	ດອກໄມ້
to follow	tạam	ຕາມ

Follow me!		
tạam khàwy		ຕາມຂ້ອຍ

food	ạa-hǎan	ອາຫານ
food poisoning	ạa-hǎan pẹn phít	ອາຫານເປັນພິດ
football (soccer)	bạan-té	ບານເຕະ
foreign	taang pá-thêht	ຕ່າງປະເທດ
foreigner	khón taang pá-thêht	ຄົນຕ່າງປະເທດ
forever	tá-làwt kạan	ຕະຫລອດການ
to forget	léum	ລືມ

I forgot.		
khàwy léum		ຂ້ອຍລືມ

to forgive	hài ạ-phái	ໃຫ້ອະໄພ
formal	tháang kạan	ທາງການ
fragile	kheuang tàek ngaai	ເຄື່ອງແຕກງ່າຍ
free (gratis)	hài lâa	ໃຫ້ລ້າ
free (not bound)	ít-sá-la	ອິດສະລະ
to freeze	sae khǎeng	ແຊ່ແຂງ
fresh	sót	ສົດ
friend	pheuan	ເພື່ອນ
friendly	pheuan mit	ເພື່ອນມິດ
full	tẹm	ເຕັມ
fun	muan	ມ່ວນ
funny	tá-lók	ຕະຫຼົກ

G

game	kạan lìin	ການຫຼິ້ນ
garbage	khìi yèua	ຂີ້ເຫຍື້ອ
garden	sŭan	ສວນ
gas (cooking)	ɑai kàet	ອາຍແກັສ
gas (petrol)	nâm-mán àet-sáng	ນ້ຳມັນແອັດຊັງ
gate	pá-tụu	ປະຕູ
generous	êua-fêua	ເອື້ອເຟື້ອ
gift	khǎwng khwǎn	ຂອງຂວັນ
girl	dék nyíng	ເດັກຍິງ
girlfriend	fáen (nyíng)	ແຟນ(ຍິງ)
to give	ɑo hâi	ເອົາໃຫ້

Give me ...
ɑo hâi dae ...   ເອົາໃຫ້ແດ່ ...

I'll give you ...
já ɑo hâi jâo ...   ຈະເອົາໃຫ້ເຈົ້າ ...

glass (drinking)	jàwk	ຈອກ
glasses (spectacles)	waen tạa	ແວ່ນຕາ
to go (on foot)	pại (nyaang)	ໄປ (ຍ່າງ)

I'm going to ... (do something)
khàwy já ...   ຂ້ອຍຈະ ...

I'm going to ... (somewhere)
khàwy já pại ...   ຂ້ອຍຈະໄປ ...

Are you going there?
jâo sii pại hàn baw   ເຈົ້າຊິໄປຫັ້ນບໍ່

God	pha-jâo	ພະເຈົ້າ
good	dịi	ດີ
government	lat-thá-bạan	ລັດຖະບານ
greedy	mak dài	ມັກໄດ້

to grow (increase)	khá-nyǎai	ຂະຫຍາຍ
to grow (produce)	pùuk	ປູກ
to guess	dao	ເດົາ
guide	pha-nak-ngaan nám thiaw	ພະນັກງານນຳທ່ຽວ
guidebook	pêum nám thiaw	ປື້ມນຳທ່ຽວ
guilty	ká-thám phít	ກະທຳຜິດ
guitar	ki-tạa	ກິຕາ

H

hair	phǒm	ຜົມ
hairdresser	saang sǒem sǔay	ຊ່າງເສີມສວຍ
half	khoeng	ເຄິ່ງ
handbag	ká-pạo hìu	ກະເປົາຫິ້ວ
handicapped person	khón phi-kạan	ຄົນພິການ
handicrafts	hát-thá-kạm	ຫັດຖະກຳ
handsome	ngáam	ງາມ
happy	dịi-jại	ດີໃຈ

Happy Birthday!	
súk-sǎn wán kòet	ສຸກສັນວັນເກີດ

hard (difficult)	nyàak	ຫຍາກ
hard (not soft)	khǎeng	ແຂງ
to hate	sáng	ຊັງ
to have	míi	ມີ

I have ...	
khàwy míi ...	ຂ້ອຍມີ ...
You have ...	
jào míi ...	ເຈົ້າມີ ...
Do you have ...?	
jào míi ... baw	ເຈົ້າມີ ... ບໍ່

he	láo	ລາວ
health	sú-khá-phâap	ສຸຂະພາບ
health centre	sǔun á-náa-mái	ສູນອະນາໄມ
to hear	dâi-nyín	ໄດ້ຍິນ
heat	khwáam hâwn	ຄວາມຮ້ອນ
heater	kheuang het hài un	ເຄື່ອງເຮັດໃຫ້ອຸ່ນ
heavy	nák	ໜັກ
hello	sá-bąi diį	ສະບາຍດີ
help	khwáam suay lěua	ຄວາມຊ່ວຍເຫຼືອ
to help	suay	ຊ່ວຍ

Can I help (you)?
míi nyǎng hài suay baw   ມີຫຍັງໃຫ້ຊ່ວຍບໍ່

Help!
sûay dae   ຊ່ວຍແດ່

here	yuu nìi	ຢູ່ນີ້
high	sǔung	ສູງ
hill	phúu	ພູ
to hire (someone)	jâang	ຈ້າງ

I'd like to hire him.
khàwy yàak jâang láo   ຂ້ອຍຢາກຈ້າງລາວ

| to hire (rent) | sao | ເຊົ່າ |

I'd like to hire it.
khàwy yàak sao   ຂ້ອຍຢາກເຊົ່າ

holiday (religious)	wán bųn	ວັນບຸນ
holiday (vacation)	wán phak wîak	ວັນພັກວຽກ
on holiday	pąi thiaw	ໄປທ່ຽວ
school holidays	wán phak hían	ວັນພັກຮຽນ
holy	sák-sít	ສັກສິດ
home	héuan	ເຮືອນ
homeland	ma-tú-phúum	ມະຕຸພູມ

homosexual (adj)	mak phêht dịaw-kạn	ມັກເພດດຽວກັນ
homosexual	khón mak	ຄົນມັກເພດດຽວກັນ
	phêht dịaw-kạn	
honest	seu-sát	ຊື່ສັດ
hope	khwáam wăng	ຄວາມຫວັງ
to hope	wăng	ຫວັງ
hospital	hóhng măw	ໂຮງໝໍ
hospitality	kạan tàwn hap	ການຕ້ອນຮັບ
hot	hâwn	ຮ້ອນ
hot (weather)	ạa-kàat hâwn	ອາກາດຮ້ອນ
hot (spicy)	phét	ເຜັດ
hotel	hóhng háem	ໂຮງແຮມ
hotel room	hàwng phak	ຫ້ອງພັກໂຮງແຮມ
	hóhng háem	
house	héuan	ເຮືອນ
housework	wiak heuan	ວຽກເຮືອນ
how	náew-dại	ແນວໃດ

How do I get to ...?
khàwy já pại hâwt ...
dài náew-dại
ຂ້ອຍຈະໄປຮອດ ...
ໄດ້ແນວໃດ

How are you?
jâo sá-bại dịi baw ...
ເຈົ້າສະບາຍດີບໍ່ ...

How much is/are ...?
láa-kháa thao dại ...
ລາຄາເທົ່າໃດ ...

human	ma-nut	ມະນຸດ
hungry	hĩu khào	ຫິວເຂົ້າ

I'm hungry.
khàwy hĩu khào
ຂ້ອຍຫິວເຂົ້າ

Are you hungry?
jâo hĩu khào baw
ເຈົ້າຫິວເຂົ້າບໍ່

to hurry	fào	ຟ້າວ
I'm in a hurry. khàwy fào		ຂ້ອຍຟ້າວ
to hurt	jép	ເຈັບ
My ... hurts. khàwy jép ...		ຂ້ອຍເຈັບ ...
husband	phŭa	ຜົວ

I

I	khàwy	ຂ້ອຍ
ice	nàm kàwn	ນ້ຳກ້ອນ
with ice	sai nàm kàwn	ໃສ່ນ້ຳກ້ອນ
without ice	baw sai nàm kàwn	ບ່ໃສ່ນ້ຳກ້ອນ
ice cream	ká-láen	ກະແລ້ມ
icon	qa-nu-săwn	ອານຸສອນ
idea	náew khwáam khít	ແນວຄວາມຄິດ
identification	bát pá-jam tua	ບັດປະຈຳຕົວ
if	thàa waa	ຖ້າວ່າ
ill	khài	ໄຂ້
illegal	phít kót-măai	ຜິດກົດໝາຍ
imagination	jín-tá-náa-kąan	ຈິນຕະນາການ
imitation	khăwng pawm	ຂອງປອມ
immediately	thán thii	ທັນທີ
import	sĭn khàa khăa khào	ສິນຄ້າຂາເຂົ້າ
to import	kąan nám khào	ການນຳເຂົ້າ
important	săm-khán	ສຳຄັນ
impossible	pęn pai baw dài	ເປັນໄປບ່ໄດ້
imprisonment	tít khuk	ຕິດຄຸກ
in	nái	ໃນ
included	pá-kàwp dûay	ປະກອບດ້ວຍ
inconvenient	baw sá-dùak	ບ່ສະດວກ
industry	út-săa-há-kąm	ອຸດສາຫະກຳ

infectious	tít sêua	ຕິດເຊື້ອ
infection	kąan tít sêua	ການຕິດເຊື້ອ
informal	baw pęn tháang kąan	ບໍ່ເປັນທາງການ
information	khàw múun	ຂໍ້ມູນ
injection	kąan sák yáa	ການສັກຢາ
injury	bàat jép	ບາດເຈັບ
insect repellent	yáa kąn máeng mái	ຢາກັນແມງໄມ້
inside	pháai nái	ພາຍໃນ
insurance	pá-kąn phái	ປະກັນໄພ
to insure	pá-kąn	ປະກັນ

It's insured.
pá-kąn lâew ປະກັນແລ້ວ

intelligent	sá-làat	ສະຫລາດ
interested	sŏn-jai	ສົນໃຈ
interesting	pęn tąa sŏn-jai	ເປັນຕາສົນໃຈ
international	la-waang sàat	ລະຫວ່າງຊາດ
Internet	in-tǫe-naet	ອິນເຕີແນັດ
Internet cafe	in-tǫe-naet kąa-féh	ອິນເຕີແນັດກາເຟ
invitation	bát sóen	ບັດເຊີນ

J

jail	khuk	ຄຸກ
jazz	tǫn-tįi jàet	ດົນຕິແຈສ
jeans	sòng yíin	ສົ້ງຢີນ
jewellery	kheuang pá-dáp	ເຄື່ອງປະດັບ
job	wiak	ວຽກ
joke	khwáam yâwk	ຄວາມຢອກ

I'm joking.
khàwy wâo yâwk ຂ້ອຍເວົ້າຢອກ

journey	dǫen tháang	ເດິນທາງ
juice (fruit)	nàm màak mái	ນ້ຳໝາກໄມ້
justice	khwáam nyu-tí-thám	ຄວາມຍຸຕິທຳ

K

key	ká-jae	ກະແຈ
to kill	khàa	ຂ້າ
kind	jai dii	ໃຈດີ
king	jâo sii-wit	ເຈົ້າຊີວິດ
kiss	kaan jùup	ການຈຸບ
to kiss	jùup	ຈຸບ
knapsack	baa-lóh	ບາໂລ
to know (a person)	húu-ják	ຮູ້ຈັກ

I know him.	
khàwy húu-ják láo	ຂ້ອຍຮູ້ຈັກລາວ

| to know (something) | húu | ຮູ້ |

L

lake	năwng	ໜອງ
land	phaen din	ແຜ່ນດິນ
landslide	din thá-lom	ດິນຖະຫລົ່ມ
language	pháa-săa	ພາສາ
large	kwăang/nyai	ກ້ວາງ/ໃຫຍ່
last (in a series)	sút-thâi	ສຸດທ້າຍ
last (as in 'last week')	kawn	ກ່ອນ
late	sâa	ຊ້າ
to be late	máa sâa	ມາຊ້າ

I'm late!	
khàwy máa sâa	ຂ້ອຍມາຊ້າ

| later | tạwn lăng | ຕອນຫລັງ |
| to laugh | hŭa | ຫົວ |

Don't laugh!	
yaa hŭa	ຢ່າຫົວ

| laundry (washing) | sak kheuang | ຊັກເຄື່ອງ |

L

laundry (place)	hóhng sak kheuang	ໂຮງຊັກເຄື່ອງ
law	kót-mǎai	ກົດໝາຍ
lawyer	nak kót-mǎai	ນັກກົດໝາຍ
lazy	khâan	ຄ້ານ
to learn	hían	ຮຽນ

I want to learn Lao.
khàwy yàak hían pháa-sǎa láo — ຂ້ອຍຢາກຮຽນພາສາລາວ

| to leave (depart) | àwk; àwk jàak | ອອກ; ອອກຈາກ |

The flight leaves at ...
thìaw bin àwk wéh-láa ... — ຖ້ຽວບິນອອກເວລາ ...

What time does the bus leave?
lot méh àwk ják móhng — ລົດເມອອກຈັກໂມງ

We're leaving for Vientiane tonight.
khéun nîi phûak háo já
àwk pai wíeng jan — ຄືນນີ້ພວກເຮົາຈະ
ອອກໄປວຽງຈັນ

to leave (behind)	pá-wǎi	ປະໄວ້
lecturer	wi-tha-nyáa-kạwn	ວິທະຍາກອນ
left (not right)	bêuang sâi	ເບື້ອງຊ້າຍ
on/to the left	tháang sâi	ທາງຊ້າຍ
legal	thèuk kót-mǎai	ຖືກກົດໝາຍ
less	nàwy-kwaa	ໜ້ອຍກ່ວາ
letter	jót-mǎai	ຈົດໝາຍ
liar	khón khìi tua	ຄົນຂີ້ຕົວະ
lice	hǎo	ເຫົາ
life	síi-wit	ຊີວິດ
lift (elevator)	lip (khân dại fái fâa)	ລິບ (ຂັ້ນໄດໄຟຟ້າ)
light (not heavy)	bạo	ເບົາ
light	fái	ໄຟ
lighter (cigarette)	káp fái	ກັບໄຟ
like (similar)	khéu	ຄື

to like	mak	ມັກ
I like ...		
khàwy mak ...		ຂ້ອຍມັກ ...
Do you like ...?		
jào mak ... baw		ເຈົ້າມັກ ... ບໍ່
line	sèn seu	ເສັ້ນຊື້
to listen	fáng	ຟັງ
Listen to me.		
fáng khàwy		ຟັງຂ້ອຍ
little (dimension)	nàwy	ໜ້ອຍ
little (quantity)	nàwy	ໜ້ອຍ
to live	qa-săi yuu	ອາໄສຢູ່
I live in ...		
khàwy yuu ...		ຂ້ອຍຢູ່ ...
Where do you live?		
jào yuu săi		ເຈົ້າຢູ່ໃສ
local	thâwng thin	ທ້ອງຖິ່ນ
lock	lái/kqwn	ໄລ/ກອນ
long	nyáo	ຍາວ
long ago	tae dọn	ແຕ່ດົນ
to look	boeng	ເບິ່ງ
to look for	sàwk hăa	ຊອກຫາ
to lose	sĭa	ເສຍ
I've lost my money.		
khàwy het ngóen sĭa		ຂ້ອຍເຮັດເງິນເສຍ
to lose (one's way)	lŏng tháang	ຫຼົງທາງ
I'm lost.		
khàwy lŏng tháang		ຂ້ອຍຫຼົງທາງ
lost (adj, things)	sĭa hăai	ເສຍຫາຍ
loud	dạng	ດັ່ງ

M

love	khwáam hak	ຄວາມຮັກ
to love (be fond of)	mak	ມັກ
to love (relationships)	hak	ຮັກ

I love you.
khàwy hak jâo | ຂ້ອຍຮັກເຈົ້າ

luck	sôhk	ໂຊກ
lucky	míi sôhk	ມີໂຊກ
luggage	ká-pao	ກະເປົາ
lunch	qa-hǎan thiang	ອາຫານທ່ຽງ

M

machine	kheuang ják	ເຄື່ອງຈັກ
mad (crazy)	bâa	ບ້າ
made (of)	phá-lit dohy	ຜະລິດໂດຍ
mail	jot-mǎai	ຈົດໝາຍ
main	sǎm-khán	ສຳຄັນ
majority	suan nyai	ສ່ວນໃຫຍ່
to make	het	ເຮັດ

Did you make it?
jâo het baw | ເຈົ້າເຮັດບໍ່

man	phùu sáai	ຜູ້ຊາຍ
many	lǎai	ຫລາຍ
map	phǎen-thii	ແຜນທີ່
market	ta-làat	ຕະຫລາດ
at the market	yuu ta-làat	ຢູ່ຕະຫລາດ
marriage	kan taeng-ngáan	ການແຕ່ງງານ
to marry	taeng-ngáan	ແຕ່ງງານ

I'm married.
khàwy taeng-ngáan lâew | ຂ້ອຍແຕ່ງງານແລ້ວ

| massage | nûat | ນວດ |

matches	káp-khìit	ກັບຂີດ
maybe	bang thii	ບາງທີ
medicine	yáa	ຢາ
to meet (someone)	phop	ພົບ

I'll meet you.
khàwy já phop jâo

ຂ້ອຍຈະພົບເຈົ້າ

| to meet (each other) | phop kạn | ພົບກັນ |

Let's meet!
phop kạn thaw

ພົບກັນເທາະ

menu	láai-kạan ạa-hǎan	ລາຍການອາຫານ
message	khàw-khwáam	ຂໍ້ຄວາມ
milk	nâm nóm	ນ້ຳນົມ
million	lâan	ລ້ານ
mind	jít jại	ຈິດໃຈ
to mind (to object)	baw hěn dịi	ບໍ່ເຫັນດີ

Do you mind ...?
... pẹn nyǎng baw

... ເປັນຫຍັງບໍ່

Never mind!
baw pẹn nyǎng

ບໍ່ເປັນຫຍັງ

mineral water	nâm háe thâat	ນ້ຳແຮທາດ
minute	náa-thii	ນາທີ
to miss (someone)	khit hàwt	ຄິດຮອດ
mistake	khwáam phít	ຄວາມຜິດ
to make a mistake	het phít	ເຮັດຜິດ

You've made a mistake.
jâo het phít

ເຈົ້າເຮັດຜິດ

to mix	pá-sǒm kạn	ປະສົມກັນ
modern	thán sá-mǎi	ທັນສະໄໝ
money	ngóen	ເງິນ
month	dẹuan	ເດືອນ

monument	á-nu-săa-wa-líi	ອະນຸສາວະລີ
more (of something)	ìik	ອີກ
morning	tawn sáo	ຕອນເຊົ້າ
mountain	phúu dawy	ພູດອຍ
mountain-climbing	khèun phúu	ຂຶ້ນພູ
mother	mae	ແມ່
movie	húup ngáo	ຮູບເງົາ

Let's see a movie.
pai boeng húup ngáo — ໄປເບິ່ງຮູບເງົາ

museum	phi-phit-tha-phán	ພິພິດທະພັນ
music	don-tii	ດິນຕີ
musician	nak-don-tii	ນັກດິນຕີ

N

| name | seu | ຊື່ |

My name is ...
khàwy seu ... — ຂ້ອຍຊື່ ...

What's your name?
jào seu nyăng — ເຈົ້າຊື່ຫຍັງ

national park	sŭan út-thi-nyáan	ສວນອຸດທິຍານ
nature	thám-ma-sàat	ທຳມະຊາດ
near (prep)	kâi	ໄກ້
nearby	yuu kâi	ຢູ່ໄກ້
necessary	jam-pen	ຈຳເປັນ
need	tâwng-kaan	ຕ້ອງການ

I need ...
khàwy tâwng-kaan ... — ຂ້ອຍຕ້ອງການ ...

We need ...
háo tâwng-kaan ... — ເຮົາຕ້ອງການ ...

O

neither ... nor	baw ... lěu	ບໍ່ ... ຫຼື
never	baw khóei	ບໍ່ເຄີຍ
new	mai	ໃໝ່
news	khao	ຂ່າວ
newspaper	năng-sěu phím	ໜັງສືພິມ
next	taw pại	ຕໍ່ໄປ
night	khám	ຄ່ຳ
no	baw	ບໍ່
noise	sǐang dạng	ສຽງດັງ
noisy	song sǐang dạng	ສົ່ງສຽງດັງ
north	něua	ເໜືອ
nothing	baw mǐi nyǎng	ບໍ່ມີຫຍັງ
not yet	nyáng	ຍັງ

We aren't in Vientiane yet.
phûak háo nyáng baw   ພວກເຮົາຍັງ
than hâwt wieng jạn   ບໍ່ທັນຮອດວຽງຈັນ

now	dịaw-nîi	ດຽວນີ້

O

obvious	thii hûu kạn dịi	ທີ່ຮູ້ກັນດີ
occupation	ǫa-sîip	ອາຊີບ
ocean	ma-hǎa-sá-mut	ມະຫາສະມຸດ
to offend	luang kǫen	ລ່ວງເກີນ
to offer	ǫo hài	ເອົາໃຫ້
office	hàwng kǫan	ຫ້ອງການ
often	sá-mam sá-měr	ສະໝ່ຳສະເໝີ
oil (petroleum)	nâm-mán	ນ້ຳມັນ
oil (vegetable)	nâm-mán phêut	ນ້ຳມັນພືດ
OK	tók-lóng	ຕົກລົງ

old	kae/thâo	ແກ່/ເຖົ້າ
Olympic Games	kí-láa oh-láem-pík	ກິລາໂອແລມປິກ
on (location)	yuu thóeng	ຢູ່ເທິງ
on (a particular day)	thii	ທີ່
once	theua dįaw	ເທື່ອດງວ
once more	iik theua neung	ອິກເທື່ອໜຶ່ງ
once (upon a time)	tae kawn	ແຕ່ກ່ອນ
one	neung	ໜຶ່ງ
one-way	thiaw dįaw	ຖ້ຽວດຽວ
only	thao-nân	ເທົ່ານັ້ນ
open (adj)	pòet	ເປີດ
opinion	khwáam khit-hĕn	ຄວາມຄິດເຫັນ

In my opinion ...
tgam khwáam khit khàwy ...   ຕາມຄວາມຄິດຂ້ອຍ...

opportunity	oh-kàat	ໂອກາດ
opposite (adj)	tàek taang	ແຕກຕ່າງ
opposite (prep)	kong kan khàam	ກົງກັນຂ້າມ
or	lĕu	ຫຼື
order	khám-sang	ຄຳສັ່ງ
to order	sang	ສັ່ງ
ordinary	thám-ma-dga	ທຳມະດາ
organisation	ong-kaan ját tâng	ອົງການຈັດຕັ້ງ
to organise	ját	ຈັດ
original	tôn sá-báp	ຕົ້ນສະບັບ
other	eun	ອື່ນ
outside	tháang-nâwk	ທາງນອກ
over (prep)	yuu thóeng	ຢູ່ເທິງ
overnight	háem khéun	ແຮມຄືນ
overseas	taang pá-thêht	ຕ່າງປະເທດ

to owe	tít-nìi	ຕິດໜີ້

I owe you. khàwy tit nìi jâo		ຂ້ອຍຕິດໜີ້ເຈົ້າ
You owe me. jâo tít nìi khàwy		ເຈົ້າຕິດໜີ້ຂ້ອຍ
owner	jâo khǎwng	ເຈົ້າຂອງ

P

pack (of cigarettes)	sáwng (yáa sùup)	ຊອງ (ຢາສູບ)
package	haw	ຫໍ່
packet	sáwng	ຊອງ
padlock	ká-jae	ກະແຈ
painful	jép	ເຈັບ
painkillers	yáa kàe pùat	ຢາແກ້ປວດ
painting	hùup tâem	ຮູບແຕ້ມ
pair	khuu	ຄູ່
palace	wáng	ວັງ
paper	jîa	ເຈ້ຍ
parcel	kheuang faak	ເຄື່ອງຝາກ
parents	phaw mae	ພໍ່ແມ່
park	sǔan sǎa-tháa-la-na	ສວນສາທາລະນະ
parliament	sá-pháa phùu tháen	ສະພາຜູ້ແທນ
part	phâak suan	ພາກສ່ວນ
to participate	míi suan huam	ມີສ່ວນຮ່ວມ
participation	kąan khào huam	ການເຂົ້າຮ່ວມ
party (fiesta)	ngáan pąa-tįi	ງານປາຕີ
party (political)	phak kąan méuang	ພັກການເມືອງ
passenger	phùu dǫhy-sǎan	ຜູ້ໂດຍສານ
passport	nǎng-sěu phaan dąen	ໜັງສືຜ່ານແດນ
path	tháang nyaang	ທາງຍ່າງ

to pay	jaai	จ่าย
peace	săn-tí-phâap	ສັນຕິພາບ
people (crowd)	fŭng són	ຝູງຊົນ
people (nation)	pá-sáa-són	ປະຊາຊົນ
perfect (adj)	sŏm-buun	ສົມບູນ
permanent	thăa-wáwn	ຖາວອນ
permission	kạan á-nu-mat	ການອະນຸມັດ
with your permission	á-nu-mat jàak jâo	ອະນຸມັດຈາກເຈົ້າ
permit	bại á-nu-nyâat	ໃບອະນຸຍາດ
to permit	á-nu-nyâat	ອະນຸຍາດ
persecution	kạan lóng thôht	ການລົງໂທດ
person	khón	ຄົນ
personal	suan tụa	ສ່ວນຕົວ
personality	ní-săi	ນິໄສ
petrol	nâm-mán àet-sáng	ນ້ຳມັນແອັດຊັງ
pharmacy	hâan khăai yáa	ຮ້ານຂາຍຢາ
phone book	pêum thóh-la-sáp	ປຶ້ມໂທລະສັບ
photograph	hûup thaai	ຮູບຖ່າຍ
to photograph	thaai hûup	ຖ່າຍຮູບ

| Can I take a photograph? khàw thaai hûup dâi baw | ຂ້ອຍຖ່າຍຮູບໄດ້ບໍ່ |

piece	pìang	ປ່ຽງ
place	bawn	ບ່ອນ
plant	phêut	ພືດ
plate	jaan	ຈານ
play (theatre)	la-kháwn	ລະຄອນ
to play	lìn	ຫຼິ້ນ

| Please. ká-lu-náa | ກະລຸນາ |

plenty	lăai	ຫຼາຍ
poetry	ká-wíi	ກະວີ
to point (with one's finger)	sǐi méu	ຊີ້ມື
police	tạm-lùat	ຕຳຫຼວດ
politics	kạan-méuang	ການເມືອງ
pollution	món-la-phit	ມົນລະພິດ
pool (swimming)	sa lǎwy nâm	ສະລອຍນ້ຳ
poor	thuk-jọn	ທຸກຈົນ
port	thaa héua	ທ່າເຮືອ
positive (certain)	nae jại	ແນ່ໃຈ

I'm positive.
khàwy nae jại   ຂ້ອຍແນ່ໃຈ

postage stamp	sá-tạem	ສະແຕມ
postcard	bát pại-sá-níi	ບັດໄປສະນີ
post code	la-hát pại-sá-níi	ລະຫັດໄປສະນີ
post office	hàwng-kạan pại-sa-níi	ຫ້ອງການໄປສະນີ
pottery (items)	kheuang pàn dịn phǎo	ເຄື່ອງປັ້ນດິນເຜົາ
pottery (place)	bawn phá-lit kheuang pàn dịn phǎo	ບ່ອນຜະລິດເຄື່ອງ ປັ້ນດິນເຜົາ
poverty	khwáam thuk-jọn	ຄວາມທຸກຈົນ
power (strength)	pha-láng	ພະລັງ
power (political)	ạm-nâat	ອຳນາດ
practical	sing thii pẹn pại dâi	ສິ່ງທີ່ເປັນໄປໄດ້
prayer	khám á-thi-thǎan	ຄຳອະທິຖານ
to prefer	mák	ມັກ

I prefer ...
khàwy mák ...   ຂ້ອຍມັກ ...

| pregnant | thěu pháa | ຖືພາ |

present (now)	pá-jú-bạn	ປະຈຸບັນ
present (gift)	khǎwng khwǎn	ຂອງຂວັນ
president	pá-tháan pá-thêht	ປະທານປະເທດ
pretty	ngáam	ງາມ
prevent	pạwng-kạn	ປ້ອງກັນ
price	láa-kháa	ລາຄາ
priest	khún phaw	ຄຸນພໍ່
prime minister	náa-yok	ນາຍົກ
prison	khuk	ຄຸກ
prisoner	nak-thôht	ນັກໂທດ
private	èh-ká-són	ເອກະຊົນ
probably	àat-já	ອາດຈະ
problem	pạn-hǎa	ປັນຫາ
procession	khá-bụan	ຂະບວນ
to produce	phá-lit	ຜະລິດ
professional	méu ɑa-sîip	ມືອາຊີບ
profit	kạm-lái	ກໍາໄລ
promise	kạan sǎn-nyáa	ການສັນຍາ
to promise	sǎn-nyáa	ສັນຍາ
prostitute	sǒh-phéh-níi	ໂສເພນີ
to protect	pạwng-kạn	ປ້ອງກັນ
protest	kạan pá-thúang	ການປະທ້ວງ
to protest	pá-thúang	ປະທ້ວງ
public	khǎwng sǎa-tháa-la-na	ຂອງສາທາລະນະ
public (adj)	sǎa-tháa-la-na	ສາທາລະນະ
in public	bawn sǎa-tháa-la-na	ບ່ອນສາທາລະນະ
to pull	dẹung	ດຶງ
to push	nyûu	ຍູ້
to put	wáang/sai	ວາງ/ໃສ່

Q

quality	khún-na-phàap	ຄຸນມະພາບ
of good quality	khún-na-phàap dịi	ຄຸນມະພາບດີ
question	khám thăam	ຄຳຖາມ
queue	khíu/thăew	ຄິວ/ແຖວ
quick (adj)	wái	ໄວ
quickly	wái	ໄວ
quiet (adj)	ngîap	ງຽບ

R

race (contest)	kạan khaeng-khăn	ການແຂ່ງຂັນ
racist	khón jam-nâek phĭu phán	ຄົນຈຳແນກຜິວພັນ
radio	wi-tha-nyu	ວິທະຍຸ
railway	tháang lot fái	ທາງລົດໄຟ
by rail	dọhy lot fái	ໂດຍລົດໄຟ
rain	fŏn	ຝົນ

It's raining.
fŏn tók   ຝົນຕົກ

rape	kha-dịi khom khĕun	ຄະດີຂົ່ມຂືນ
to rape	khom khĕun	ຂົ່ມຂືນ
rare (unusual)	hăa nyàak	ຫາຍາກ
raw	díp	ດິບ
razor blades	bại-mĩit thăe	ໃບມິດແຖ
to read	aan	ອ່ານ
ready	phàwm lâew	ພ້ອມແລ້ວ
reason	săa-het	ສາເຫດ
receipt	bại hap ngóen	ໃບຮັບເງິນ
recently	qa-dịit phaan pại baw dọn	ອາດິດຜ່ານໄປບໍ່ດົນ
to recommend	nae-nám	ແນະນຳ

refrigerator	tûu yén	ຕູ້ເຢັນ
refugee	óp-pha-nyop	ອົບພະຍົບ
refund	tháen khéun	ແທນຄືນ
refuse	khìi nyèua	ຂີ້ເຫຍື້ອ
to refuse	pá-tí-sèht	ປະຕິເສດ
region	khŏng-khèht	ຂົງເຂດ
registered letter	jót-măai long tha-bian	ຈົດໝາຍລົງທະບຽນ
regulation	kót la-bìap	ກົດລະບຽບ
relationship	khwáam sǎm-phán	ຄວາມສຳພັນ
to relax	phak phawn	ພັກຜ່ອນ
religion	sàat-sá-nǎa	ສາສະໜາ
to remember	jeu	ຈື່
remote	thu-la kạn-dạan	ທຸລະກັນດານ
rent	khaa sao	ຄ່າເຊົ່າ
to rent	sao	ເຊົ່າ
to repair	pạeng	ແປງ
to repeat	wâo mai	ເວົ້າໃໝ່

Please repeat that.
ká-lu-náa wâo mai   ກະລຸນາເວົ້າໃໝ່

representative	tụa tháen	ຕົວແທນ
republic	sǎa-tháa-la-na-lat	ສາທາລະນະລັດ
reservation	kạan sang-jạwng	ການສັ່ງຈອງ
reserve	sá-ngǔan	ສະຫງວນ
to reserve	sang-jạwng	ສັ່ງຈອງ
respect	khwáam kháo-lop	ຄວາມເຄົາລົບ
to respect	kháo-lop	ເຄົາລົບ
responsibility	khwáam hap-phit-sâwp	ຄວາມຮັບຜິດຊອບ
rest (relaxation)	kạan phak-phawn	ການພັກຜ່ອນ
to rest	phak-phawn	ພັກຜ່ອນ
restaurant	hâan ạa-hǎan	ຮ້ານອາຫານ

to return	káp	ทับ
We'll return on ...		
phûak háo ja káp ...		ພວກເຮົາຈະກັບ ...
return ticket	pîi pại-káp	ປີ້ໄປກັບ
rich	hang	ຣັ່ງ
right (not left)	bêuang khwǎa	ເບື້ອງຂວາ
on/to the right	tháang khwǎa	ທາງຂວາ
right (correct)	thèuk	ຖືກ
I'm right.		
khàwy thèuk		ຂ້ອຍຖືກ
risk	siang	ສ່ຽງ
river	mae nâm	ແມ່ນ້ຳ
road	tháang	ທາງ
robber	nak-pûn	ນັກປຸ້ນ
robbery	kạan pûn	ການປຸ້ນ
roof	lǎng-kháa	ຫຼັງຄາ
room (general)	hàwng	ຫ້ອງ
room (hotel)	hàwng phak	ຫ້ອງພັກ
rope	sêuak	ເຊືອກ
round	wóng món	ວົງມົນ
rubbish	khìi nyèua	ຂີ້ເຫຍື້ອ
ruins	sàak sá-lak-hak-pháng	ສາກສະລັກຮັກພັງ
rule	la-bìap	ລະບຽບ

S

sad	sào	ເສົ້າ
safe (adj)	pàwt-phái	ປອດໄພ
safe	tûu sep	ຕູ້ເຊັບ
safely	dûay khwáam pàwt-phái	ດ້ວຍຄວາມປອດໄພ
safety	khwáam pàwt-phái	ຄວາມປອດໄພ
same	khéu-kạn	ຄືກັນ

to say	wâo	ເວົ້າ
I said ... khàwy dài wâo ...		ຂ້ອຍໄດ້ເວົ້າ ...
Can you say that again? jâo wâo mai dâi baw		ເຈົ້າເວົ້າໃໝ່ໄດ້ບໍ່
scenery	thíu-that	ທິວທັດ
school	hóhng hían	ໂຮງຮຽນ
secret (adj)	lap	ລັບ
secret	khwáam lap	ຄວາມລັບ
to see	hěn	ເຫັນ
I see. (understand) khàwy khào jai		ຂ້ອຍເຂົ້າໃຈ
I see (it). khàwy hěn		ຂ້ອຍເຫັນ
selfish	hěn kae tụa	ເຫັນແກ່ຕົວ
to sell	khǎai	ຂາຍ
Do you sell ...? jâo khǎai ... baw		ເຈົ້າຂາຍ ... ບໍ່
to send	song	ສົ່ງ
sentence (grammar)	pá-yòhk	ປະໂຫຍກ
serious	nák-nǎa	ໜັກໜາ
several	lǎai	ຫຼາຍ
shade	hom	ຮົ່ມ
share	hùn	ຫຸ້ນ
to share	baeng kạn	ແບ່ງກັນ
she	láo	ລາວ
shoes	kòep	ເກີບ
shop	hâan khâa	ຮ້ານຄ້າ
short (length, duration)	sàn	ສັ້ນ
a short time ago	waang mǎw mǎw níi	ຫວ່າງໝໍໆນີ້
short (height)	tîa	ເຕ້ຍ

shortage	**khàat khŏen**	ຂາດເຂີນ
to shout	**hâwng**	ຮ້ອງ
to show	**sá-dąeng**	ສະແດງ

Show me, please.
ąo hài khàwy boeng dae — ເອົາໃຫ້ຂ້ອຍເບິ່ງແຕ່

shut (adj)	**pít lâew**	ປິດແລ້ວ
to shut	**pít**	ປິດ
shy	**ąai**	ອາຍ
sick	**khài**	ໄຂ້
sickness	**lôhk**	ໂລກ
sign	**pàai**	ປ້າຍ
signature	**láai sén**	ລາຍເຊັນ
similar	**khàai khéu kąn**	ຄ້າຍຄືກັນ
since (from that time)	**tang tae**	ຕັ້ງແຕ່
since (because)	**neuang jàak waa**	ເນື່ອງຈາກວ່າ
single (unmarried)	**sòht**	ໂສດ
sister	**nâwng săo**	ນ້ອງສາວ
to sit	**nang**	ນັ່ງ

Sit down.
nang lóng — ນັ່ງລົງ

situation	**sá-phâap-kąn**	ສະພາບການ
size	**khá-nàat**	ຂະໜາດ
sleep	**kąn náwn**	ການນອນ
to sleep	**náwn**	ນອນ

I'm asleep.
khàwy kąm-láng náwn — ຂ້ອຍກຳລັງນອນ

He's asleep.
láo náwn lap — ລາວນອນລັບ

Are you asleep?
jâo náwn lap baw — ເຈົ້ານອນລັບບໍ່

sleepy	hĭu náwn	ທ້ຽວນອນ

I'm sleepy.
khàwy hĭu náwn — ຂ້ອຍທ້ຽວນອນ

slow	sâa	ຊ້າ
slowly	sâa	ຊ້າ
small	nâwy	ນ້ອຍ
smell	kin	ກິ່ນ
to smell	dọm	ດົມ
snow	hí-ma	ຫິມະ
soap	sá-bụu	ສະບູ
solid (adj)	năa nâen; khăeng	ໜາແໜ້ນ; ແຂງ
some	bạang	ບາງ
someone	bạang khón	ບາງຄົນ
something	bạang yaang	ບາງຢ່າງ
sometimes	bạang khàng	ບາງຄັ້ງ
son	lùuk sáai	ລູກຊາຍ
song	phéhng	ເພງ
so-so	thám-ma-dạa	ທຳມະດາ
soon	nái wái-wái nîi	ໃນໄວໆນີ້

Sorry!
khăw thôht — ຂໍໂທດ

south	tâi	ໃຕ້
souvenir	khăwng khwăn	ຂອງຂວັນ
to speak	wâo	ເວົ້າ
special	phi-sèht	ພິເສດ
spirits (alcohol)	lào	ເຫຼົ້າ
sport	kí-láa	ກິລາ
spring (season)	la-dụu bạan mai	ລະດູບານໃໝ່
square	já-tú-lat	ຈະຕຸລັດ

stairway	khàn dại	ຂັ້ນໄດ
stamp	sá-tạem	ສະແຕມ
standard (adj)	mâat-tá-thǎan	ມາດຕະຖານ
station (bus)	sá-thǎa-níi (lot)	ສະຖານີ (ລົດ)
stay	kạan phak háem	ການພັກແຮມ
to stay	phak	ພັກ

I'll stay here for (two days).
khàwy já phak yuu níi (sǎwng mêu) ຂ້ອຍຈະພັກຢູ່ນີ້ (ສອງມື້)

to steal	lak	ລັກ

My money has been stolen.
ngóen khàwy thèuk lak ເງິນຂ້ອຍຖືກລັກ

stop	bawn jàwt	ບ່ອນຈອດ
to stop	yut	ຍຸດ
storey	sǎn	ຊັ້ນ
ground floor	sǎn lum	ຊັ້ນລຸ່ມ
storm	pháa-nyu	ພາຍຸ
story	ni-tháan	ນິທານ
straight	seu	ຊື່
straight ahead	seu pại	ຊື່ໄປ
strange	pàek	ແປກ
stranger	khón pàek nàa	ຄົນແປກໜ້າ
street	thá-nǒn	ຖະໜົນ
on strike	pá-thùang	ປະທ້ວງ
strong	khǎeng háeng	ແຂງແຮງ
student	nak-séuk-sǎa	ນັກສຶກສາ
stupid	ngoh	ໂງ່
suddenly	ká-than-hǎn	ກະທັນທັນ
suitcase	ká-pao	ກະເປົາ
summer	la-dụu hàwn	ລະດູຮ້ອນ
sun	tạa-wén	ຕາເວັນ

sure (certain)	nae jai	ແນ່ໃຈ

Are you sure?
jâo nae jai baw — ເຈົ້າແນ່ໃຈບໍ່

I'm sure.
khàwy nae jai — ຂ້ອຍແນ່ໃຈ

surname	náam sá-kun	ນາມສະກຸນ
surprise	pá-làat jai	ປະຫລາດໃຈ
sweet	wǎan	ຫວານ
sweets (candy)	khào-nǒm	ເຂົ້າໜົມ
to swim	láwy nâm	ລອຍນ້ຳ

T

table	tó	ໂຕະ
to take	qo	ເອົາ

I'll take one.
khàwy já qo qn neung — ຂ້ອຍຈະເອົາອັນໜຶ່ງ

Can I take this?
khàwy qo qn nìi dâi baw — ຂ້ອຍເອົາອັນນີ້ໄດ້ບໍ່

to talk	wâo	ເວົ້າ
tall	sǔung	ສູງ
tasty	sâep	ແຊບ
tax	pháa-sǐi	ພາສີ
taxi	lot thaek-sǐi	ລົດແທກຊີ
teacher	náai khúu	ນາຍຄູ
telephone	thóh-la-sáp	ໂທລະສັບ
to telephone	thóh-la-sáp	ໂທລະສັບ
telephone book	pêum thóh-la-sáp	ປຶ້ມໂທລະສັບ
temperature	un-na-phúum	ອຸນນະພູມ
tent	phàa tên	ຜ້າເຕັ້ນ

| to thank | khǎw khàwp jai | ຂໍຂອບໃຈ |

| Thank you. | | |
| khàwp jai | | ຂອບໃຈ |

theatre	hóhng la-kháwn	ໂຮງລະຄອນ
there	yuu hàn	ຢູ່ຫັ້ນ
they	phùak khǎo	ພວກເຂົາ
thick	nǎa	ໜາ
thief	john	ໂຈນ
thin	bạang	ບາງ
to think	khit	ຄິດ
thirst	hǐw nâm	ຫິວນ້ຳ

| I'm thirsty. | | |
| khàwy hǐw nâm | | ຂ້ອຍຫິວນ້ຳ |

| ticket | pîi | ປີ້ |
| time | wéh-láa | ເວລາ |

What time is it?		
wéh-láa ják móhng		ເວລາຈັກໂມງ
I don't have time.		
khàwy baw mii wéh-láa		ຂ້ອຍບໍ່ມີເວລາ

timetable	táa-láang wéh-láa	ຕາລາງເວລາ
tin opener	kheuang khǎi ká-pạwng	ເຄື່ອງໄຂກະປ໋ອງ
tip (gratuity)	ngóen thip	ເງິນທິບ
tired	meuay	ເໝື່ອຍ
today	mêu-nii	ມື້ນີ້
together	phàwm kạn	ພ້ອມກັນ
toilet	hàwng nâm	ຫ້ອງນ້ຳ
toilet paper	jìa hàwng nâm	ເຈັ້ຍຫ້ອງນ້ຳ
tomorrow	mêu-eun	ມື້ອື່ນ
tonight	khéun nii	ຄືນນີ້

too (also)	dùay	ດ້ວຍ
too (as in 'too hot')	phôht	ໂພດ
tooth	khàew	ແຂ້ວ
torch (flashlight)	fái săai	ໄຟສາຍ
to touch	jáp	ຈັບ
to tour	thawng thiaw	ທ່ອງທ່ຽວ

I'm touring Laos.
khàwy kạm-láng thawng   ຂ້ອຍກຳລັງທ່ອງ
thiaw yuu pá-thêht láo   ທ່ຽວຢູ່ປະເທດລາວ

tourist	nak thawng thiaw	ນັກທ່ອງທ່ຽວ
towards	thŏeng	ເຖິງ
towel	phàa set tọh	ຜ້າເຊັດໂຕ
town	méuang	ເມືອງ
track (path)	tháang	ທາງ
in transit	dọen tháang phaan	ເດີນທາງຜ່ານ
to translate	pạe	ແປ
translation	kạan pạe	ການແປ
trekking	dọen paa	ເດີນປ່າ
trip	thìaw	ທ່ຽວ
true	thèuk tàwng	ຖືກຕ້ອງ
to trust	seua	ເຊື່ອ
to try (attempt)	pha-nyáa-nyáam	ພະຍາຍາມ
to try (taste food)	síim	ຊີມ
to try on (clothing)	láwng nung kheuang	ລອງນຸ່ງເຄື່ອງ
TV	thóh-la-that	ໂທລະທັດ

U

umbrella	khán hom	ຄັນຮົ່ມ
uncomfortable	baw sá-dùak	ບໍ່ສະດວກ
under	tâi/ kàwng	ໃຕ້/ກ້ອງ

| to understand | khào jai | ເຂົ້າໃຈ |

| I don't understand. khàwy baw khào jai | | ຂ້ອຍບໍ່ເຂົ້າໃຈ |
| Do you understand? jâo khào jai baw | | ເຈົ້າເຂົ້າໃຈບໍ່ |

unemployed	wàang ngáan	ຫວ່າງງານ
university	ma-hăa-wi-tha-nyáa-lái	ມະຫາວິທະຍາໄລ
unsafe	baw pàwt-phái	ບໍ່ປອດໄພ
until	jon thóeng	ຈົນເຖິງ
up	khèun	ຂຶ້ນ
upstairs	sân thóeng	ຊັ້ນເທິງ
urgent	duan	ດ່ວນ
useful	pęn pá-nyòht	ເປັນປະໂຫຍດ
useless	baw míi pá-nyòht	ບໍ່ມີປະໂຫຍດ

V

vacation (holiday)	phak tháang kąan	ພັກທາງການ
vaccination	sak-yáa-pàwng-kąn lôhk	ຊັກຢາປ້ອງກັນໂລກ
in vain	het tae baw dài hap phǒn	ເຮັດແຕ່ບໍ່ໄດ້ຮັບຜົນ
valuable	míi khaa	ມີຄ່າ
value	láa-kháa	ລາຄາ
various	sing taang-taang	ສິ່ງຕ່າງໆ
vegetable garden	sŭan phák	ສວນຜັກ
vegetarian (person)	khón kịn jęh	ຄົນກິນເຈ
vegetarian (adj)	jęh	ເຈ
very	lăai	ຫຼາຍ
video	wíi-dịi-ǫh	ວິດິໂອ
view	thíu-thát	ທິວທັດ
village	muu bân	ໝູ່ບ້ານ
visa	wi-sáa	ວິຊາ
to visit	nyîam-nyáam	ຢ້ຽມຢາມ

to vomit	hâak	ຮາກ
to vote	lêuak tàng	ເລືອກຕັ້ງ

W

to wait	láw thàa	ລຳຖ້າ

Wait a moment!
thàa béut neung — ຖ້າບຶດໜຶ່ງ

waiter	dék sòep	ເດັກເສີບ
walk	nyaang	ຍ່າງ

Do you want to go for a walk?
jào yàak pai nyaang liin baw — ເຈົ້າຢາກໄປຍ່າງ ຫຼິ້ນບໍ

to walk	nyaang	ຍ່າງ
to want	tâwng-kaan/yàak	ຕ້ອງການ/ຢາກ

I want ...
khàwy tâwng-kaan ... — ຂ້ອຍຕ້ອງການ ...

We want ...
phûak háo tâwng-kaan ... — ພວກເຮົາຕ້ອງການ ...

Do you want ...?
jào tâwng-kaan ... baw — ເຈົ້າຕ້ອງການ ... ບໍ

war	sŏng-kháam	ສົງຄາມ
warm	óp-un	ອົບອຸ່ນ
to wash (oneself)	àap-nâm	ອາບນ້ຳ

I have to wash (bathe).
khàwy tâwng àap-nâm — ຂ້ອຍຕ້ອງອາບນ້ຳ

to wash (clothes)	sak	ຊັກ
to wash (other objects)	lâang	ລ້າງ
watch	kaan duu-láe	ການດູແລ
to watch	boeng	ເບິ່ງ

Watch out!
la-wáng — ລະວັງ

water	nâm	ນ້ຳ

way	tháang	ທາງ
Which way?		
tháang dại		ທາງໃດ
WC	hàwng nâm	ຫ້ອງນ້ຳ
we	phûak háo	ພວກເຮົາ
wealthy	hang míi	ຮັ່ງມີ
weather	qa-kàat	ອາກາດ
wedding	ngáan taeng-ngáan	ງານແຕ່ງງານ
week	qa-thit	ອາທິດ
Welcome!		
nyín dịi tâwn hap		ຍິນດີຕ້ອນຮັບ
well	nâm sàang	ນ້ຳສ້າງ
west	thit tạa-wén tók	ທິດຕາເວັນຕົກ
wet	pìak	ປຽກ
what	nyăng	ຫຍັງ
What time is it?		
jak móhng		ຈັກໂມງ
What did you say?		
jâo wâo nyăng		ເຈົ້າເວົ້າຫຍັງ
when	wéh-láa dại	ເວລາໃດ
where	yuu săi	ຢູ່ໃສ
who	phăi	ໃຜ
Who do I ask?		
khàwy ja thăam phăi		ຂ້ອຍຈະຖາມໃຜ
wife	mía	ເມຍ
to win	sa-na	ຊະນະ
window	pawng îam	ປ່ອງຢ້ຽມ
winter	la-dụu năo	ລະດູໜາວ
wise	hûu lăai	ຮູ້ຫຼາຍ
wish	kạan qa-thí-thăan	ການອາທິຖານ
to wish	qa-thí-thăan	ອາທິຖານ

with	káp	ກັບ
within	pháai-nái	ພາຍໃນ
without	pạa-sá-jàak	ປາສະຈາກ
woman	mae nyíng	ແມ່ຍິງ
wooden	het dûay mâi	ເຮັດດ້ວຍໄມ້
work	wîak	ວຽກ
to work	het wîak	ເຮັດວຽກ
world	lôhk	ໂລກ
worse (adj)	sua kwaa	ຊົ່ວກ່ວາ
worse (adv)	hâai-háeng-kwaa	ຮ້າຍແຮງກ່ວາ
write	khĭan	ຂຽນ

I'm writing ...
khàwy kạm-láng khĭan ...   ຂ້ອຍກຳລັງຂຽນ ...

She's writing ...
láo kạm-láng khĭan ...   ລາວກຳລັງຂຽນ ...

| wrong | phít phâat | ຜິດພາດ |

You're wrong.
jâo phít   ເຈົ້າຜິດ

year	pii	ປີ
two years ago	săwng pii kawn	ສອງປີກ່ອນ
yes	maen	ແມ່ນ
yesterday	mêu-wáan nîi	ມື້ວານນີ້
you (sg)	jâo	ເຈົ້າ
you (pl)	phûak jâo	ພວກເຈົ້າ
young	num	ໜຸ່ມ

Z

zone	khèht	ເຂດ
zoo	sŭan sát	ສວນສັດ
zodiac	hŏh-láa-sàat	ໂຫລາສາດ

INDEX

Phrasebooks

L onely Planet phrasebooks are packed with essential words and phrases to help travellers communicate with the locals. With colour tabs for quick reference, an extensive vocabulary and use of script, these handy pocket-sized language guides cover day-to-day travel situations.

- handy pocket-sized books
- easy to understand Pronunciation chapter
- clear & comprehensive Grammar chapter
- romanisation alongside script to allow ease of pronunciation
- script throughout so users can point to phrases for every situation
- full of cultural information and tips for the traveller

'...vital for a real DIY spirit and attitude in language learning'
– *Backpacker*

'the phrasebooks have good cultural backgrounders and offer solid advice for challenging situations in remote locations'
– *San Francisco Examiner*

Arabic (Egyptian) • Arabic (Moroccan) • Australian *(Australian English, Aboriginal and Torres Strait languages)* • Baltic States *(Estonian, Latvian, Lithuanian)* • Bengali • Brazilian • Burmese • British *(English, dialects, Scottish Gaelic, Welsh)* • Cantonese • Central Asia *(Kazakh, Kyrgyz, Pashto, Tajik, Tashkorghani, Turkmen, Uyghur, Uzbek & others)* • Central Europe *(Czech, German, Hungarian, Polish, Slovak, Slovene)* • Costa Rica Spanish • Czech • Eastern Europe *(Albanian, Bulgarian, Croatian, Czech, Hungarian, Macedonian, Polish, Romanian, Serbian, Slovak, Slovene)* • East Timor *(Tetun, Portuguese)* • Egyptian Arabic • Ethiopian *(Amharic)* • Europe *(Basque, Catalan, Dutch, French, German, Greek, Irish, Italian, Maltese, Portuguese, Scottish Gaelic, Spanish, Turkish, Welsh)* • Farsi *(Persian)* • Fijian • French • German • Greek • Hebrew • Hill Tribes *(Lahu, Akha, Lisu, Mong, Mien & others)* • Hindi/Urdu • Indonesian • Italian • Japanese • Korean • Lao • Latin American Spanish • Malay • Mandarin • Mongolian • Moroccan Arabic • Nepali • Papua New Guinea • Pidgin • Pilipino (Tagalog) • Polish • Portuguese • Quechua • Russian • Scandinavian *(Danish, Faroese, Finnish, Icelandic, Norwegian, Swedish)* • South-East Asia *(Burmese, Indonesian, Khmer, Lao, Malay, Tagalog Pilipino, Thai, Vietnamese)* • South Pacific *(Fijian, Hawaiian, Kanak languages, Maori, Niuean, Rapanui, Rarotongan Maori, Samoan, Tahitian, Tongan & others)* • Spanish *(Castilian, also includes Catalan, Galician & Basque)* • Sri Lanka • Swahili • Thai • Tibetan • Turkish • Ukrainian • USA *(US English, vernacular, Native American, Hawaiian)* • Vietnamese

COMPLETE LIST OF LONELY PLANET BOOKS

AFRICA Africa on a shoestring • Cairo • Cape Town • East Africa • Egypt • Ethiopia, Eritrea & Djibouti • The Gambia & Senegal • Healthy Travel Africa • Kenya • Malawi • Morocco • Mozambique • Read This First: Africa • South Africa, Lesotho & Swaziland • Southern Africa • Southern Africa Road Atlas • Tanzania, Zanzibar & Pemba • Trekking in East Africa • Tunisia • Watching Wildlife East Africa • Watching Wildlife Southern Africa • West Africa • World Food Morocco • Zimbabwe, Botswana & Namibia

AUSTRALIA & THE PACIFIC Aboriginal Australia & the Torres Strait Islands • Auckland • Australia • Australia Road Atlas • Bushwalking in Australia • Cycling Australia • Cycling New Zealand • Fiji • Healthy Travel Australia, NZ and the Pacific • Islands of Australia's Great Barrier Reef • Melbourne • Micronesia • New Caledonia • New South Wales & the ACT • New Zealand • Northern Territory • Outback Australia • Out to Eat – Melbourne • Out to Eat – Sydney • Papua New Guinea • Queensland • Rarotonga & the Cook Islands • Samoa • Solomon Islands • South Australia • South Pacific • Sydney • Sydney Condensed • Tahiti & French Polynesia • Tasmania • Tonga • Tramping in New Zealand • Vanuatu • Victoria • Walking in Australia • Watching Wildlife Australia • Western Australia

CENTRAL AMERICA & THE CARIBBEAN Bahamas, Turks & Caicos • Baja California • Bermuda • Central America on a shoestring • Costa Rica • Cuba • Dominican Republic & Haiti • Eastern Caribbean • Guatemala • Guatemala, Belize & Yucatán: La Ruta Maya • Havana • Healthy Travel Central & South America • Jamaica • Mexico • Mexico City • Panama • Puerto Rico • Read This First: Central & South America • World Food Mexico • Yucatán

EUROPE Amsterdam • Amsterdam Condensed • Andalucía • Austria • Barcelona • Belgium & Luxembourg • Berlin • Britain • Brussels, Bruges & Antwerp • Budapest • Canary Islands • Central Europe •Copenhagen • Corfu & the Ionians • Corsica • Crete • Crete Condensed • Croatia • Cycling Britain • Cycling France • Cyprus • Czech & Slovak Republics • Denmark • Dublin • Eastern Europe • Edinburgh • England • Estonia, Latvia & Lithuania • Europe on a shoestring • Finland • Florence • France • Frankfurt Condensed • Georgia, Armenia & Azerbaijan • Germany • Greece • Greek Islands • Hungary • Iceland, Greenland & the Faroe Islands • Ireland • Istanbul • Italy • Krakow • Lisbon • The Loire • London • London Condensed • Madrid • Malta • Mediterranean Europe • Milan, Turin & Genoa • Moscow • Mozambique • Munich • The Netherlands • Normandy • Norway • Out to Eat – London • Paris • Paris Condensed • Poland • Portugal • Prague • Provence & the Côte d'Azur • Read This First: Europe • Rhodes & the Dodecanese • Romania & Moldova • Rome • Rome Condensed • Russia, Ukraine & Belarus • Scandinavian & Baltic Europe • Scotland • Sicily • Slovenia • South-West France • Spain • St Petersburg • Sweden • Switzerland • Trekking in Spain • Tuscany • Venice • Vienna • Walking in Britain • Walking in France • Walking in Ireland • Walking in Italy • Walking in Spain • Walking in Switzerland • Western Europe • World Food France • World Food Ireland • World Food Italy • World Food Spain

COMPLETE LIST OF LONELY PLANET BOOKS

INDIAN SUBCONTINENT Bangladesh • Bhutan • Delhi • Goa • Healthy Travel Asia & India • India • Indian Himalaya • Karakoram Highway • Kerala • Mumbai (Bombay) • Nepal • Pakistan • Rajasthan • Read This First: Asia & India • South India • Sri Lanka • Tibet • Trekking in the Indian Himalaya • Trekking in the Karakoram & Hindukush • Trekking in the Nepal Himalaya

ISLANDS OF THE INDIAN OCEAN Madagascar &Comoros • Maldives • Mauritius, Réunion & Seychelles

MIDDLE EAST & CENTRAL ASIA Bahrain, Kuwait & Qatar • Central Asia • Dubai • Iran • Israel & the Palestinian Territories • Istanbul • Istanbul to Cairo on a Shoestring • Istanbul to Kathmandu • Jerusalem • Jordan • Lebanon • Middle East • Oman & the United Arab Emirates • Syria • Turkey • World Food Turkey • Yemen

NORTH AMERICA Alaska • Boston • Boston Condensed • British Colombia • California & Nevada • California Condensed • Canada • Chicago • Deep South • Florida • Great Lakes • Hawaii • Hiking in Alaska • Hiking in the USA • Honolulu • Las Vegas • Los Angeles • Louisiana & The Deep South • Miami • Montreal • New England • New Orleans • New York City • New York City Condensed • New York, New Jersey & Pennsylvania • Oahu • Out to Eat – San Francisco • Pacific Northwest • Puerto Rico • Rocky Mountains • San Francisco • San Francisco Map • Seattle • Southwest • Texas • Toronto • USA • Vancouver • Virginia & the Capital Region • Washington DC • World Food Deep South, USA • World Food New Orleans

NORTH-EAST ASIA Beijing • China • Hiking in Japan • Hong Kong • Hong Kong Condensed • Hong Kong, Macau & Guangzhou • Japan • Korea • Kyoto • Mongolia • Seoul • Shanghai • South-West China • Taiwan • Tokyo • World Food – Hong Kong

SOUTH AMERICA Argentina, Uruguay & Paraguay • Bolivia • Brazil • Buenos Aires • Chile & Easter Island • Colombia • Ecuador & the Galapagos Islands • Healthy Travel Central & South America • Peru • Read This First: Central & South America • Rio de Janeiro • Santiago • South America on a shoestring • Santiago • Trekking in the Patagonian Andes • Venezuela

SOUTH-EAST ASIA Bali & Lombok • Bangkok • Cambodia • Hanoi • Healthy Travel Asia & India • Ho Chi Minh City • Indonesia • Indonesia's Eastern Islands • Jakarta • Java • Laos • Malaysia, Singapore & Brunei • Myanmar (Burma) • Philippines • Read This First: Asia & India • Singapore • South-East Asia on a shoestring • Thailand • Thailand's Islands & Beaches • Thailand, Vietnam, Laos & Cambodia Road Atlas • Vietnam • World Food Thailand • World Food Vietnam

Also available; Journeys travel literature, illustrated pictorials, calendars, diaries, Lonely Planet maps and videos. For more information on these series and for the complete range of Lonely Planet products and services, visit our website at **www.lonelyplanet.com**.